THE DOORS OF AYAHUASCA

Gerardo Prat

The Doors of Ayahuasca

Three Experiences that Can Transform Pain

SucoPress Publishing

This publication is written with the intention of sharing a positive personal experience for the author. It does not seek to replace the diagnosis or treatment of a medical or professional therapist and does not advocate for any illegal activities. Any application of the content of these pages is at the sole discretion and risk of the reader. The author and editor assume no responsibility for any actions taken now or in the future. Names and some characteristics have been changed to protect the identity of individuals. While the intention of this book is to provide reliable information on the subject matter, it is sold with the understanding that neither the author nor the editor are recommending, suggesting, advising, or advocating for the use of ayahuasca or any other substance or therapy. Laws regarding possession, carrying, and use of substances vary depending on each state, country, or territory. It is recommended that anyone interested in these practices consult a duly authorized and certified medical professional or therapist, and seek professional therapeutic advice before trying any substance mentioned in this publication. The author, editor, and publisher assume no responsibility incurred or derived from the use, interpretation, or application of the content of this book.

Prat, Gerardo
The Doors of Ayahuasca, Three Experiences that can Transform Pain / Gerardo Prat. – 1st ed. – Los Angeles, California.
234 p. ; 23 x 15 cm.

ISBN: 9798879019278

1. Self-growth 2. Self Help. 3. Personal Experiences.

© 2024, Gerardo Prat
Imprint: SucoPress, Inc Publishing

All Righs reserved.

Print in USA

No part of this publication, including the cover design, may be reproduced, stored, or transmitted in any form or by any means, electronic, chemical, mechanical, optical, recording, or photocopying, without prior permission from the publisher.

Contents

INTRODUCTION 13
   Why not be afraid of it? 15
   Why respect it? 16

PART I 19
The Expanded Mind…Indeed! 19
The Connection with my Inner Wise Self 19
   FIRST INTAKE OF AYAHUASCA 21
   A distant beginning 21
   Hyper-control or responsible preparation? 23
   The First Week of the Rest of My Life 25
   The First *Day* of the Rest of My Life 27
   The Long Hugs 28
   The Ceremony 29
   From Hyper-control to Surrender 31
   The Inner Voice 34
   Fear; a tunnel to the next level 35
   The Chieftain 36
   If This Is Being a Victim… 37
   The Last Tunnel 39
   The Total Expansiveness 39
   An Image of our Universe 41
   Healing the Body 43
   Healing the Tree 44
   That Voice, again 45
   The sadness of humanity 47

Finally...gratitude 48
LESSONS FROM THE FIRST EXPERIENCE 49
PART II 54
A Family Constellation in the Universe 54
The Connection with Others 54
SECOND INTAKE OF AYAHUASCA 55
A deeper understanding of "magic" 55
We are all addicts... 59
One more clue… 60
A framework of psychological understanding 63
Take me 66
Night premonition? 67
A double bet... 68
A house on the hill 70
Take one.. 73
A Concert of Pain 79
Ah… Of course! 81
Seeing the Pain of Others 83
And I heard the pain of The Woman 85
And I saw the pain of Man 88
Robert de Niro's grimace 90
The yellow cry 91
And I looked at the center...................................... 95
How much pain can I expel? 97
The smoke and the fear 99
"Sit between my legs." 101
Am I made for transcendent things? 103

- The place of fear 107
- The great paradox 107
- And I peed on myself.. 110
- Yes, I'm going to *take* Mauricio 112
- To convince is not to allow growth 118
- Being Present for the Women in my Life........... 122
- Being Present for the Men in my Life 126
- Another archetype of me 129
- Healing through each other................................. 133
- The psychoanalyzed psychologist 135
- "Kid, you eat for all the hunger in Africa, hey!" 138
- Another healing to the future 144
- The bodybuilding musician 149
- Once again, the Pride.. 150
- Whose poncho is it?.. 153
- The Bear and the Squirrel 159
- An "unfinished conclusion"................................. 162
- THE INTEGRATION 165

PART III.. 169
Reaching the true choice 169
Desiring and Wanting.. 169
- THIRD INTAKE OF AYAHUASCA 171
- The Basement 171
- The third day of the rest of my life 173
- To dis-order to order... 176
- Next, I undress 177
- The Return of the Shark...................................... 178

Mom's Crying	179
The Echo of the Universe and the first election	180
The fear of homosexuality	182
The scream that dad kept inside	184
Resting is not the same as sleeping	188
The Vomit of Mom	190
And now how do I write all this?	191
The Echo of the Universe and the Second Election	194
The fear of creativity	196
Efrén wants to fly	198
The other meaning of smoke	199
The reflection of death is…	201
The Echo of the Universe and the third choice	203
Choosing from the Adult, the True... Third Choice	205
What do I do tomorrow?	207
Between wanting and desiring	209
The Choice is the Path, and I Choose to Play	211
And now, how do I tell the shaman?	213
A new sense of smoke	214
Attraction and choice	214
The vocational nurse	218
A Mirror of My Anger	220
Susan is Susana, really!	224
You never finish choosing	226
BY WAY OF CONCLUSION	228
The Result or the Process?	228

*To those who made my life more difficult,
more challenging, and who sacrificed for me.
To my wife, Susana,
who growths right next to me.
To my daughters, Emma and Alena,
whom I make life more difficult, more challenging...
To myself, who put so much effort into allowing them
to live more of their own pain and less of mine.*

*Cualquier semilla, cuando es planta, quiere ver
la misma estrella de aquel atardecer
que la salvó del pico agudo
refugiándola al oscuro
de la gaviota arrasadora de los surcos...*

León Gieco

*Any seed, when it becomes a plant, wants to see
the same star of that sunset
that saved it from the sharp beak
sheltering it in the darkness
from the seagull that ravages the furrows...*

León Gieco

Introduction

Talking about the experience of ayahuasca is not talking about a plant or a psychotropic substance; it is talking about oneself. Because although it is often called the "master plant", and many times reference is made to what it "teaches us", in reality, all that wisdom is already within us. Ayahuasca, like other substances offered by nature, is nothing more than a "key" that grants us access to that profound knowledge, dormant within us.

Used by Amazonian peoples for at least two thousand years, ayahuasca is a compound of two plants: the *banisteriopsis caapi liana* and the *chacruna* leaf. This mixture produces, in chemical terms, a hallucinogenic effect on the brain. However, the "highest" purpose of the tribes that used it was always to achieve a connection with magical worlds, an "expansion of consciousness." After long hours of cooking, and consumed in a specific dosage, this bitter brew is the centerpiece of traditional ceremonies of purification, healing and internal learning. Ayahuasca also has a power of physical detoxification, stemming from the organic composition of the plant.

The magical drug is also the indigenous counterpart to Western scientific medicine. It is administered by the shaman, a spiritual guide who enjoys, within the tribe, a prestige similar to that of the doctor or psychotherapist in our Occidental society.

Dimethyltryptamine (a psychoactive entheogen better known as DMT) is the natural biosynthesis of the drug in this Amazonian potion and has been the subject of numerous studies by scholars and scientists. One of them, the physician Rick Strassman, conducted research with numerous laboratory tests on patients to whom he administered the drug. In his book *DMT: The Spirit Molecule*, Strassman cites a key revelation from one of his patients named Philip:

The trance Philip referred to –he writes– *is what we now call "the psychedelic threshold" of DMT. One crosses it when one perceives a separation between consciousness and the body, and the psychedelic effects completely replace the normal content of the mind.*

I add, always according to my experience, that the mind remains present during this trip, but... "to the side"; ready in case one needs it, but without intruding or blocking the experience.

After fifteen to forty minutes of having drunk it, the psychological structure becomes sensitized; the body numbs (though without losing muscular control); one enters a dreamlike journey where dreams are real and reality is like a dream; profound revelations and understandings occur within the Self. And I emphasize that these kinds of epiphanies are, in reality, profound understandings of personal truths that live within us; they swim in the sea of our experience and wisdom, as if waiting to be discovered. These understandings are not at all typical of recreational drugs. Neither are encounters with the deepest fears or even that kind of "death in life" that many experience.

There is no convention regarding the effects of ayahuasca: each person has a different experience; even the same person can have different experiences from one ceremony to another. However, most testimonies agree that despite how terrifying the journey can be after ingestion, the overall balance ends up being unequivocally positive. Many of those who claim to have had a "bad experience" often admit not having approached the ceremony with proper preparation, including fasting, spiritual cleansing, a sense of purpose, detoxification from food and other drugs or medications.

Ayahuasca, precisely because of the intricacies of the experience, is not a drug that generates addiction. In fact, almost all participants in these ceremonies will agree that it takes a lot of courage to delve into or revisit this universe. Many, like this author, need to wait almost a year to experience it again. Far from *creating* an addiction (and according to abundant testimonial evidence), the master plant helps *correct* multiple types of addictions. Many cautiously say that it is not advisable for people suffering from bipolar disorders or cases of psychosis. But what ayahuasca requires is not fear; it's respect.

Why not be afraid of it?

This question is a bit tricky. On one hand, the plant may confront us with our greatest and deepest fears. And to embark on that journey, one must be courageous; there's no doubt about that. However, on the other hand, it's like when you get on one of those impressive roller coasters at amusement parks, the real danger is usually very, very low. The fear is "controlled." We know that beyond a bit of dizziness or vomiting (which, by the way, is one of the most common effects immediately after ingesting the plant), nothing bad is going to happen to us.

In the case of ayahuasca, something similar happens, but here it's our Inner Wise One who "controls" the situation. Therefore, even though one might go through the most intense and even horrifying journey into the depths of the unconscious, "Mother" or "Grandmother" –as ayahuasca is also called– will not demand more than our body can handle. It will not reveal more than our soul can grasp at that precise moment in our lives. So, it is our own Inner Wise Self who regulates the intensity and magnitude of the experience.

According to known reports, there are very few fatalities related to ayahuasca consumption, and in most cases, the person had ingested it together with other drugs or alcohol, often for recreational purposes. Remember that preparation both in terms of the body (through a prior diet) and the soul is essential, along with a humble purpose of healing and self-knowledge.

Due to the so-called "ayahuasca tourism," which is currently very popular in Perú and other areas of the Amazon, there have been some cases of overdose in recent years, usually administered by fake shamans more guided by greed than by the spirit. However, we should not let ourselves be influenced by a few cases, no matter how real and unfortunate they may be. Should we avoid taking ibuprofen because more than a hundred people die daily from analgesic overdoses in the United States alone? After all, there is a basic principle of chemistry that states that any substance can be toxic and dangerous depending on the dose and frequency of ingestion. Even H2O (yes, drinking water) can be deadly if consumed in excessive amounts.

Why respect it?

Because wisdom, without sufficient spiritual and psychological preparation, can be mere information; without the appropriate interpretation, the benefit of deep self-knowledge would be lost. Therefore, from our perspective, it is fundamental that this experience is *part of a personal development and psychological therapy process, and that it is approached with a sincere purpose of self-discovery.*

As for the legality of ayahuasca consumption, it depends on the practice and the territory. In the United States, where the compound DMT is considered a "Schedule I" substance, its cultivation, possession, sale, and transportation are prohibited. However, in countries like Italy (as well as in traditionally used countries like Brazil, Mexico, or Perú) these four practices are legal and, in many cases, promoted in prolific spiritual retreats. In Spain, there is a legal hybrid: all uses are allowed, under certain controls, except for public sale.

The truth is that legality is a matter of time. As mentioned earlier, academic medicine is discovering the therapeutic contribution of hallucinogenic drugs such as ayahuasca and mushrooms. There is growing scientific evidence of the healing effects of these once-prohibited potions on some illnesses that modern medicine cannot cure.

Beyond controls and prohibitions, what happens with these drugs is that traditional medical institutions, out of convenience or ignorance, do not recognize them. As a consequence, they remain outside the legal circuit, but the practices are so healing that nothing stops them. There's no need to go to the Amazon. Genuine groups conduct these practices in private and controlled environments. Enthusiasts of self-discovery access these beautiful and profound experiences, as in my case, in cities like Los Angeles or Madrid (my apologies to purists who believe that ayahuasca should only be taken in the Amazon, as if potatoes, originally from the Americas, didn't taste good in an Irish-style stew).

Therefore, just as recently happened with marijuana in the United States, it is almost inevitable that in the coming years, the medicinal use of these natural substances will be recognized and legalized. In fact, their therapeutic effects are currently being studied at prestigious universities like Oxford or Harvard. And it is highly likely that, in a few years, this gift from *Pachamama* (or some derivative of DMT) will become another therapeutic tool to combat diseases such as depression and addiction. In my opinion, this will be highly positive, but only if two circumstances are met: that control does not end up in the hands of the unscrupulous and profitable pharmaceutical industry, and that the practice does not limit itself to mere recreational use.

I have taken "recreational drugs" on a few occasions. I have always been very conservative about it. And on this path of discovery (as I will develop further later), I learned that drugs are neither good nor bad. It primarily depends on the purpose for which they are taken. And that purpose, intention, is the great dividing line.

The main problem with drugs is that people use them for fun and to escape their pain, to **dis-connect** from a painful reality.

The most genuine purpose, on the other hand, is to **connect**. And the goal: to elevate self-knowledge. Both are essential for anyone who wants to embark on this path. That was precisely one of the revelations of my first experience with ayahuasca.

PART I

The Expanded Mind...Indeed!
The Connection with my Inner Wise Self

FIRST INTAKE OF AYAHUASCA

DECEMBER 21, 2019

Our fears stem from our traumas and then take root in our attachments; attachment to what we have or what we want to have. But fear can be a path for salvation. When we look squarely at what scares us, when we let it in, when we open our hearts to it and surrender to it, we realize that our fear was nothing more than a door. A flower that, when opened, transforms into a tunnel leading to the next screen of the "video game of life." In this first trip, fear manifested itself to me as a shark.

A distant beginning

Eleven years before writing these lines, during a Latin Grammy event that I was covering as a journalist in the city of Las Vegas, I met Carlos, a Latin music producer. He was friendly and spoke slowly. Carlos asked me if I was interested in having him tell me about a meeting that was going to take place in the Nevada desert. Somewhat distrustful, I asked him if it was not one of those semi-fraudulent pyramid business schemes (to which we have all been invited at some point) and he assured me that it was not. He invited me because he had noticed that I was a "seeker of self-knowledge."

I met him in a café near the strip, the main street where the luminous hyperrealism of the casinos moves away, with each flash, from the true "illumination."

Long minutes of conversation had passed, and Carlos still didn't tell me what the meeting was about. I must admit that his proposal had intrigued me. He even mentioned that famous artists, like Alejandro Sanz, had attended those "ceremonies".

Seeing that I wouldn't go into the middle of the desert without more information, Carlos decided to reveal his secret: he was inviting me to a ceremony that included the ingestion of peyote.

Peyote, or *Lophophora williamsii*, is a spineless cactus that has a hallucinogenic effect similar to that of ayahuasca. Its origin, however, is different, as it mainly grows in the deserts of northern Mexico and the southwest of the United States of America. We could say, at the risk of being too simplistic, that it is the Mexican version of ayahuasca.

Until that moment, I had never heard anything about that mysterious cactus. But my caution, at that time, was more powerful than my intrigue, and Carlos received a kind "no."

My reaction was curious because rational caution and a deep desire to face my fears coexist in me. That time, caution won. But it wouldn't be for long.

Almost a decade later, my wife, Susana, and I met a Spanish couple, Marta and Sergio, who, like us, are very involved with alternative therapies and personal development. With them, we spent time playing board games and relaxing in deep jacuzzi conversations.

It was in one of those conversations that Marta spoke for the first time about "Mother." She had done several ceremonies of ayahuasca some time ago, and the story of her experiences seduced my exploring soul. It was she who also told me that the experience can be like "living death", or delving into the deepest of our fears. Also that, once the journey begins, "one cannot control what the plant is going to teach you", and that, regardless of whether one tries to learn something specific in one intake, the plant –or, as I later discovered, our Inner Wise Self– will only teach us what we need to learn at that precise moment in our lives. And that's what it's all about: taking action on what demands attention.

Just as the human body, if we take care of it and do not contaminate it with unhealthy foods, possesses the wisdom and power to heal itself, our Inner Being, if we cultivate the spirit and self-awareness, holds the almost absolute power to give us knowledge. Body and spirit, then, automatically tend toward health and homeostasis, self-regulation, and balance. Of course, if we authorize them. And permission simply consists of not contaminating them, respectively, with "junk" food or with "junk" thoughts.

The thought of losing control was difficult for me. But at that moment, while listening to Marta, I knew that such a step would be inevitable for me.

Hyper-control or responsible preparation?

Each time I return to my homeland, Argentina, I usually delve into some new therapy or revisit personal work to progress in my evolution as a human being.

Since my teenage years, my aunt Ana has been a sort of spiritual guide for me, opening doors to various therapies and techniques, expanding my understanding and exploration. These could be as diverse as meditation in a labyrinth or reciting a mantra from Sai Baba. It was my aunt Ana, the eccentric one (whom I remember standing on her head against the wall when I was four years old, at a time when yoga was considered extravagant), who convinced my parents to take me to psychological therapy at the age of six or seven when they were going through a divorce.

She was also the one who, at the age of fifteen, when I ended up in the hospital due to a senseless fight with a pizza maker that left a cut on my hand, sat with me in a café in Buenos Aires and said, "You are seeking self-harm. Do you know where self-harm leads if you don't stop it? Towards death."

I would soon discover that Ana had not exaggerated; within the next two years, two boys from my inner circle of friends would take their own lives. Eric ended his life at the age of eighteen by shooting himself, and a few months later, Federico followed suit, succumbing to carbon monoxide poisoning. It's possible he might have survived had his unconscious mind not chosen a different path.

It was then that Ana introduced me to Alfredo Szymanis, the first therapist I willingly chose to see. Since that moment, the deepest personal mission of my life has been self-awareness. My goals from those adolescent years are very simple: I just wanted and want to suffer less and be a better person.

At over eighty years old, Ana continues to guide me through the pathways of self-healing. Thus, during the two decades I have lived in Los Angeles, every time I have returned to Argentina, I have undertaken some spiritual retreat or Family Constellations session with her.

It was this "preparation" (in this game of life where avoiding pain seems easier than accepting it) that gave me the confidence to experiment with ayahuasca for the first time, which I did in Spain, the home country of my wife.

The First Week of the Rest of My Life

I must admit that this "responsible preparation" for self-awareness coexists within me with an instinctive need to control the situation. But this time, I managed to combine both factors, and during one of my trips to Madrid, I scheduled a comprehensive "healing itinerary." This helped ensure that my first experience with ayahuasca was –after some challenges– wonderful and pleasant (because the journey with "Grandmother" can also be both wonderful and harrowing).

In this plan, my schedule looked like this:

Monday: Consultation with Sergio Martín, a "kinesiologist" who works with Chinese medicine.

Tuesday: Free.

Wednesday: Appointment with Manuel Márquez, a famous quantum numerologist.

Thursday: Meeting with Ascensión, an elderly woman who, like a "computed tomography" of the future, can scan the patient's unconscious and simply reveal what one hides from oneself.

Finally, on Saturday, after a twenty-four-hour fast, I would travel to the Sierra de Madrid, to a rural house where the ayahuasca ceremony would take place. José Luis, the shaman recommended by my friend Marta, whom I had contacted a month earlier from Los Angeles, had made a space for me in the weekend gathering.

While we flew to Madrid almost every year to visit Susana's family, I had never met the kinesiologist, the numerologist, the clairvoyant, or that shaman, to whom I would entrust my mind and being. But all the preparation of that week, combined with that of my entire life, would be crucial in my first contact with the master plant. I review some key points.

In addition to the valuable physical-emotional assessment by the kinesiologist, numerology was extremely revealing. In summary, Manuel pointed out two fundamental things: that I possessed the identity of the Master (my quantum number is 9) and that I did not master my "low masculine energy," which corresponds to everything related to weakness, mediocrity, error, clumsiness (concepts that are neutral in themselves, neither positive nor negative). By not mastering it, he emphasized, I judged that "low masculine energy" as "bad," both in myself and in others. By not accepting it and judging it, I allowed the *invasion* of other people or circumstances into my life. And that was the cause of all my problems. If I stopped judging my low masculine energy, if I accepted myself as sometimes clumsy, weak, fearful, mediocre, I could better achieve my life purpose.

From the entire experience with Manuel, I would hope that at least the concept of "allowing oneself to be *invaded*" remains with the reader, as it would later appear in the ayahuasca ritual.

The meeting with Ascensión (Ascension, in English –a name loaded with meaning) provided other aspects strictly personal, which would also emerge, amalgamated, during that night in the Sierra de Madrid. Among other things, the sweet elderly woman told me that I had the energy of a Spiritual Teacher, of a Chief with his (my) feathered crown. I must have retained that image because it later appeared in my ayahuasca dream.

A few months before this experience, I had started a profound therapeutic process with Mauricio Weintraub, an eminent psychologist with whom I continue to work. And while Mauricio has helped me discover the basic structures of my traumas and is truly the most important guide in my life today, the truth is that, during my week in Madrid, all these strangers would channel what I had not been able to unlock in years of therapy; that which would come to me in the night of ayahuasca in the form of magic.

And it was Saturday...

The First *Day* of the Rest of My Life

My Spanish brothers-in-law, people whom I would choose as my family of origin a thousand times over, had never undergone therapy, let alone ceremonies with psychedelics. Yet, they supported my adventure with love.

On December 21, Jordi dropped me off at a gas station where, minutes later, participants in the ceremony passing through my area would pick me up; people I, of course, didn't know.

The small two-door Seat stopped at the agreed-upon gas station, and the driver, a thin man around forty-five, greeted me. The other two passengers had to get out to maneuver my suitcase into the tiny trunk, amidst bags and sleeping mats.

A few minutes after gliding down the road toward the town of Zarzalejo, I learned that the person sitting next to me was none other than José Luis, the shaman. Anyone with the prejudice that a shaman must be a guy with a Peruvian poncho and the beard of a prophet would have been a bit disappointed. I, honestly, felt comfortable. José Luis was an ordinary guy. With his colloquial speech, which could very well be that of my brother-in-law having drinks on a terrace, this Madrid shaman did not pretend to showcase any special wisdom. *And that* –I thought– *is very wise.*

The Long Hugs

After a few reflective minutes, the green-grayish mountains were already breathing their fresh and kind air over us. A passing stream welcomed us to the village, the liquid fire of the sun reflected in its waters. The entrance to the estate, of which I still have a photo, was guarded by two medieval stone columns. Beyond the iron gates, a lengthy pathway stretched into an unknown adventure.

Upon reaching the building, we parked alongside other cars. People with slow smiles began to emerge from them. Some helped unload the sleeping mats; others unloaded their small bags for a single night. I noticed that everyone greeted each other with hugs. But as I paid attention, I realized that they didn't just hug; they embraced in a way that it seemed they wouldn't let go. Arms entwined for thirty or forty seconds. It made me a bit embarrassed. *Do they really need to hug so much?* –I thought– *entangled in my prejudice.*

I knew no one. I felt foreign, strange. It also seemed like I was the only one experiencing ayahuasca for the first time — a kind of "new kid" in class.

Inside the country house, the logs in the fireplace crackled amid the murmurs of the people. The living room chairs were filled with these "students" who seemed like lifelong friends; perhaps even friends from "all lives." And it turned out that it was indeed so. There was another beginner, besides me, but even he was a friend of another "regular." Some of them, I found out later, had attended up to thirty of these ceremonies. *What an exaggeration; that seems more like an addiction than a journey of self-discovery*, I judged inwardly.

Someone opened the doors to an adjacent room. It was a hall over three hundred square feet in size. Through an old stone wall, the windows allowed the humble countryside landscape to enter. The other three walls were plastered and neatly white. At the end of the room, two digital speakers contrasted with Peruvian blankets and a couple of indigenous instruments. The wooden floor was scattered with about thirty sleeping mats. Incense and another intense, greenish aroma began to fill every inch of the air.

In December, it's very cold in the mountains; and one corner stood out from the others with a cozy *salamandra*, a blazing cast-iron stove. I chose the mat next to it. There, I founded my spot. That warmth was my long welcoming hug.

The Ceremony

Except for the poncho, José Luis still wore plainclothes. In his calm tone, he explained some guidelines, which he had already mentioned to me on the road. I'll try to remember and convey what he said, although I may not be entirely faithful to his words. After introducing his assistant, Vanessa, José Luis began:

For those who come for the first time, I'm going to tell you how we conduct our ceremony. Although there are no "rules" per se, there are things we need to consider to have a better experience. Everyone has blindfolds on the side of their sleeping mats. You also have a bucket for... you know, for vomiting if you need to. I must say that in our ceremonies, few people vomit. I don't know why, as it's not wrong to do so. By the way, in the tradition of ayahuasca ceremonies, vomiting is a form of purification. But it's not essential for the experience.

He then mentioned the plant mix that makes up ayahuasca and continued:

First, we will take a shot, –pointing to a small glass–; *that's the ayahuasca dose. In about thirty minutes, I will come around and ask each of you if you want more or if that was enough. If you want more, I'll give you another half shot. If we think it's necessary, after a while, I'll ask you again how you're doing. And if you want, we can give you rapé.*

I began to worry. *Rapé*? It was evident that everyone was familiar with it. Later, I learned that it's a stimulant well-known to many people, particularly in Spain. Traditionally, it's ground tobacco used for inhalation, but the shaman explained that in this case, it was mixed with another plant. And he demonstrated how it was ingested:

I'm going to put this powder in this horn. I'll give it to you to inhale. Rapé accelerates the ayahuasca process and allows those who find it difficult to enter the journey to do so.

Inhale! For me, who had never put anything up my nose, the mere idea alone generated prejudice.

However, in my dilemma of "preparation or hyper-control," I had carried in my mind a mantra I had learned from my aunt Ana years ago: "I Surrender, I Trust, I Accept, and I am Grateful" (like that, with each word capitalized).

That was the first small challenge. And if I wanted to do this right, I had to surrender...

From Hyper-control to Surrender

After about an hour of having taken a shot and a half of the plant, my body was completely relaxed, although my senses remained heightened. Amid the gentle incense, shamanic melodies fought for every atom of the environment; first, drum beats, and then, undulating waves of "medicine music," inspired by ancient Amazonian vibrations.

I must note that my mind functions, at times, like an Excel spreadsheet. It's a defense mechanism. My mother, when she lost her temper, was not exactly gentle with me, and my life was marked by a certain preventive guard against her "madness". A semi-permanent state of alertness, as in a "war". Therefore, in situations that are not under my absolute control, and if I don't organize myself, the fear of chaos comes over me, and the threat of catastrophe seems like an imminent slap in the face.

Two things had been recorded in that mental Excel sheet:

Cell 1: My friend Marta had told me that the "key" to ayahuasca (so to speak because there is no actual key) was surrendering to fear. People talk about facing fears. But no. With ayahuasca, it's not about facing anything. "If you want to confront something, all you're going to do is go in circles, and that's more and more pain and fear," Marta had warned me. "The key is surrendering to fear. When that great fear comes, *your* fear, your monster, you have to surrender to it, let it in." And that was my first premise.

Cell 2: Here was that mantra I had learned from my aunt: "I Surrender, I Trust, I Accept, and I am Grateful." And despite Ana repeating it like a parrot, now I confess, I had never truly understood it; until that afternoon.

Now, in my internal order of the "perfect student" and in the face of fear, I understood the lesson: I *Surrender* to this experience. I *Trust* this shaman. I will *Accept* whatever comes, even the toughest fear or the most horrible experience. And, come what may, I will be *Grateful* for it.

Although I didn't know it, this profound understanding was a sign that the plant was already working in me.

It's incredible how long it takes to assimilate the true meaning of those phrases in which masters like Gandhi, Sai Baba, or countless avatars of history condense wisdom! For example: "Non-violence is not in loving your friend but in loving your enemy," or "There are no Ways to Peace, Peace is the Way" (both by Gandhi). Or the simple verses of a poem. You understand them for their beauty and simplicity. But assimilating them is another thing.

Almost an hour had passed; but only that, time had passed. *Better nothing than the monster*, I thought from fear. *It's fine, if nothing happens. Later, I'll go and tell everyone that nothing happened to me, that it doesn't have to be, and that's it. I didn't come here to prove anything to anyone.* The cast-iron stove looked at me, making a face with its flames.

The shaman approached me with the horn and snuff in hand. He asked me softly, not to interrupt those who were already daydreaming:

—How are you doing?

—Fine... —I said—. Well, I'm super relaxed but... I don't know if it has taken effect yet.

—Do you want *rapé*?

I Surrender, I Trust, I Accept, and I am Grateful, I remembered easily, as I now deeply understood the meaning of those words.

—Yes —I replied, nodding in humble silence.

A little pile of powder fell into the shaman's hand. *All that is going to enter my nose*, I thought, frightened. I had already seen how he put the horn into one nasal cavity of others. The person inhaled and made a surprised face. Then, José Luis repeated the procedure in the remaining nasal cavity.

The shamanic music radiated a literal and absolute peace. José Luis had prepared a playlist on his Spotify, and the traditional "medicine music" of the Amazonians merged with Carmina Burana, which, in turn, intertwined with heartbeat percussions, and then entered, hand in hand with Krishnamurti, the rhythms of India.

With fear, I accepted the *invasion* of that horn into my nose.

—You're going to exhale; I'm going to blow the snuff on you, and you're going to inhale, but slowly, slowly.

—...

I saw the mountain of tobacco. In the middle of the imposing mountain range, it was a grain of sand, but immense to me. I had exhaled with so much energy and anticipation that as soon as the shaman blew into my nasal cavity, I needed to inhale forcefully. Suddenly, that part of my brain, the right side, went numb. The Excel spreadsheet laughed at me. Everything I had been controlling crumbled.

I didn't think at that moment about what the numerologist had told me just a few days ago, but boy, did I feel invaded. So much so that José Luis didn't dare proceed with the next nasal cavity. I lay down. I was no longer in control.

The cast-iron stove, which until now emitted welcoming warmth, turned into my enemy. I felt like I couldn't breathe. *What if this stove is emitting carbon monoxide?*, I thought.

I remembered Federico, that brother of my adolescence who had died from carbon monoxide poisoning, around the time the pizza maker cut my hand.

This whole place is closed. Shouldn't I go outside and breathe oxygen?

I sat up a bit, but I didn't dare. I didn't know if it was allowed to go outdoors.

I Surrender, I Trust, I Accept, and I am Grateful. Something had brought me back to the mantra, which was not enough now. I had lost control over things. I was scared... All that was left was to "surrender," let it in. I put back on the eye cover that I had taken off minutes earlier to receive the snuff. Then, I lay down on the mat.

Before the soft syllable "OM" finished exhaling in a Vedic song, other melodious words responded, vibrating: "Open your heart, open your feeling, open your understanding, set reason aside, and let the sun shine, hidden within you. Open ancient memory, hidden in the fire, in the air, in the water."

Suddenly, from one of the melodies playing on the speakers, from the very molecules of sound, celestial and aquamarine lights exploded. My surroundings transformed into an infinite greenish-blue sea...

And from here on, anyone who is not open to wonder had better leave these pages.

The Inner Voice

I am at the bottom of the sea, swimming with a group of sharks. I feel like dancing, moving through the warm water at the rhythm of these giant fish. Suddenly, one huge shark, about one and a half times my size, approaches me on my right side, its five rows of teeth exposed, its mouth wide open. In my physical reality, which I never lose sight of and can return to whenever I want (although I don't want to), I turn my head to that side. I'm on a journey to the depths of my fears. I'm scared, but not really, as if this creature weren't truly a threat. Just as it's about to reach me with its jaws open wide, the beast makes a turn. The shark doesn't bite me.

Then, it charges again, swaying in the green-blue water, coming towards me. And it still doesn't bite me. On the contrary, it aligns itself with me, swimming alongside.

Astonished, I ask:

—But... are you not going to eat me?

—No. I am your friend —it replies—, Besides, I've already eaten, I'm not hungry.

And we keep moving.

After a while, still incredulous and not fully trusting (in myself), I question it again:

—And if you were hungry... would you bite me?"

The shark turns toward me with a glance that's both mischievous and wise. It smiles. We both smile, complicit. Then, I look ahead, and...

Fear; a tunnel to the next level

...From some corner of my mind, the one that now rests aside without the obligation to work or protect me, I think: *Is this just the pitiful trip of a drug addict, tripping on a mat?* And for a moment, I feel sorry for myself.

But it's only a second until I realize that it's my mind trying to pass a desperate judgment, to invade me. And although it interrupts me for that second, I don't let myself be swayed by it.

And now, where prejudice once dwelled, a passage opens before me; one with green, white, and black lights, among others. I start to ascend rapidly through it. It's a spacious, dazzling tunnel. If I were to try to explain its beauty, I couldn't, it wouldn't fit in a poem.

I traverse it at high speed, incredibly fast, *like in a Star Wars movie*, it occurs to me.

I leave behind my motionless corporeal vessel. I travel through my third eye. And I continue ascending through the tunnel, which seems infinite.

The Chieftain

I arrive at a place somewhere in space. To save on metaphors, my mind is like... expanded. I feel the energy expanding in my forehead. I float in the eternal universe, in a trance similar to what I've sometimes felt while meditating or in a hypnosis session, but hundreds of times deeper, more encompassing.

Suddenly, I notice my body. I realize that I have my hands crossed over my head (I'm still lying on my mat the whole time) and I whispered to myself: *My intertwined fingers are like a crown of feathers or a golden crown, like that of a chieftain or a Mayan priest.* And I begin to think. I use the word "think" arbitrarily because I don't really ponder the nature of this, whether it might be a regression to another life, I don't know. I even prefer to choose that all this narrative and accumulation of images is something more self-induced, voluntary: a mixture of what one has experienced, read in books, or seen in movies, and my own internal wisdom.

The point is that, with my arms raised and hands in the shape of a crown, I am a Mayan priest slowly ascending a pyramid, step by step. The people are waiting for some kind of sacrifice; I, in some way, am avoiding sacrificing an animal or a person. And breaking tradition, I tell my people: "The true sacrifice is within you, it is the sacrifice of renouncing oneself" (I search for the word ego, renouncing the ego, but I don't know the term in this time and space), and I put my hands on my chest.

I think all of this is, again, more induced by my imagination than by the plant, by the trance itself. But the truth is that I still feel consciousness totally outside the body, to the point that the fear of staying in these worlds leads me to occasionally move my toes, to check that my body is still here.

Knowing that I can return to Earth at will reassures me, allows me to continue the journey. And another revelation comes to my Being.

If This Is Being a Victim...

I notice again my hands crossed over my head, wearing the imposing Mayan crown. But now, I realize that these hands, one over the other, can also represent those of Christ nailed to the cross. I don't like that as much as the idea of the chieftain or priest's headdress. I feel my hands, the nail piercing them; I can almost touch the roughness of the forged iron moving through.

And a thought comes to my mind: *Once again, I feel like "the victim."* I remember Manuel's words, the numerologist: "As a victim, you let yourself be invaded, you set no limits." But for a few minutes, I feel like that: weak, invaded by the nail, helpless, at the mercy of the cross. I start to feel tears; they roll, touch my ears. And that's precisely what I have to work on: the vulnerability that, like the traitors of Jesus Christ, I so harshly judge in myself. How can I surrender and accept that being a victim is neither good nor bad, but just is, period?

Then, giving another twist to reason, I think: *But if being a victim is being Christ, what a luxury of a victim!* And that's the lesson the numerologist wanted to give me. *Of cooourse!* I hear myself recite in an infinite pause. *I judge weakness, my victim part, my clumsy, lazy, mediocre, fearful side, but in reality, Jesus was a victim and a king, sacrificed and chieftain!*

Having understood the lesson, if that's possible at all right now, I find myself turning my head to my left, where a trapped breeze carries the music through the room. In that direction are the speakers, and in my immense darkness, that's where the light comes from. Until this moment, I'm having a beautiful experience, full of peace and infinite sensations. Occasionally, I peek from under the blindfold. The pacifying shamanic chords are joined by the fresh scent of some natural essence that the assistant sprays over us.

To my right, suddenly, I feel the weight of a black hole. And I think: *Uh-oh, here it is! Now comes the deep fear. There must be the dragon or the monster that appears, to each one according to their own measure, with ayahuasca.* If that's my fear, I don't want to face it. And in my twilight, I dare not look.

But as much as I want to return to the top of that Mayan pyramid or stay on the cross of that redeemed victim in me, the dense black hole is now my only present. I know it's there, to my right. I can't run away or avoid it.

And after a few moments, I tell myself:

Well, you know what? I'm going to look at the fear; I'm going to let it in, let it pass, I'm going to experience it; it's going to...

So, I turn my head to the right.

The Last Tunnel

Even though I'm almost ready to face them, there is no dragon, no monster, no ghost. Instead, there's another tunnel, a spatial void, a hole that absorbs me gently and tenderly. This time, devoid of colors, deep in its blackness; with stars, yes, but swiftly passing by my sides as I'm transported at an incalculable speed.

I ascend and ascend through the tube, but it's only my mind that rises, or rather, my Being.

My body lies motionless on the mat. It has no sensation whatsoever. Perhaps I could move my toes and return to it, but I don't want to. I leave it below, without fear, without giving it importance.

Suddenly, after several curves and counter-curves, always ascending, I exit the tunnel. A gentle bounce stops my movement. Everything halts, suspended, floating, in complete weightlessness. The stars still move, but slowly, almost imperceptibly.

The Total Expansiveness

I feel... how to explain it! Many times I've read and heard the phrase "expansion of consciousness", and I thought it was about deeply understanding how the world works, that everything is Love, that we are all the same. Well, self-awareness; maybe, even understanding beyond reason. Broadening knowledge. But, well, what I experience up here, in space, is feeling the immaterial consciousness, truly perceiving it EX-PAN-DED.

It's as if my mind spans kilometers and kilometers towards infinity; as if it's swollen in every direction, forward and backward, in an unprecedented dimension. As if, traversing it all, it is connected with space and time, forming part of the infinite and at the same time, being me... Because I'm thinking (or rather, being aware of it) that I can perceive the Entirety, the Source.

Even though reason is the vehicle, it is far inferior to this experience. This is the true Expansion, the point at which the consciousness that dwells within each of us merges with the Higher Consciousness.

It's as if (the "as if" becomes inevitable) the entire Energy of the Universe, God, the Source or whatever name one gives to that superiority, is everywhere but concentrated in small amounts in each being to form their soul.

At this moment, I understand that it is to this place we come when we die, that here is my father, my departed loved ones, my ancestors, my dog Lukie... all of them! From there, we come. And this understanding brings me peace. An inexpressible peace, resistant to words. I know that when a loved one dies, they will be permanently part of this totality, of this beautiful sensation of knowing and being part of everything. I assume that I will return here, and the fear of death completely disappears.

I deduce that, from now on, on the day someone close dies, my ego will suffer, yes, and I will miss them. I will also return to fearing my own death, fear of pain. But somewhere in my Being, this memory of having understood and inhabited this Sacred Place will remain intact.

And another clear understanding comes now.

"By understanding this, by having been in this place, I don't need to come back until I die. Because, what sense would it make to do so if we depart from here to Earth for a reason!" It's contradictory when put into words, but while I want to come back here when possible and will try to remember this place in my meditations (as one shouldn't abuse the master plant), I realize that I don't have to be here now.

The true lesson is that, once knowing this "place", I have to pour its Message and its Energy into everyday life. I suppose I will, whenever possible, infusing love into each of my daily actions. Or I'll know how! But, surely, I will have to apply it. Because this is of such magnitude that, once known, you can't let it slip away.

(An Image of our Universe)

I don't know if the scheme that follows was entirely conceived at that moment or later, but the truth is that I would like to illustrate that Sacred Place in the following way. Let's imagine three concentric circles, one inside the other. The small and inner circle, let's call it Zone 1, is our Planet. The circle that surrounds it is Zone 2. Outside of it is Zone 3. What is beyond this? Who knows!

In Zone 1, then, we are, humans, like actors in a play or a video game; embodied avatars of souls that are Pure Consciousness, and reside in Zone 3. It was precisely Manuel who told me that our Higher Beings incarnate in us to experience life. As if saying –I think with a smile– from what I describe as Zone 3: *Well, I want to taste what sushi is like.* So they choose an avatar (a body) and incarnate into it.

Let's go back to the schemeJust before incarnating, those Beings inhabit Zone 2, resembling a waiting room as they anticipate entry into the game. In this Zone 2, there are also souls that disembody (die and leave their bodies on Earth) and ascend there before returning to Zone 3.

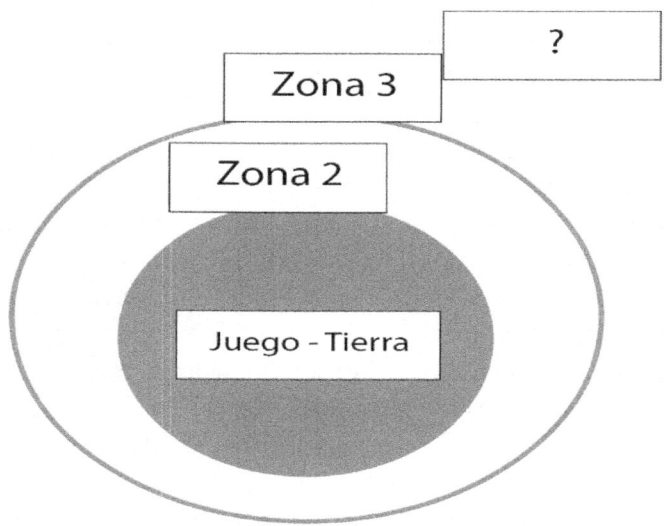

I do not intend with this to provide a description of how the spiritual world truly is or how the field of our souls works. I don't think anyone knows for certain, and perhaps those realities are not entirely describable and even less "drawable." Furthermore, if we start to delve into the understanding of quantum physics, there might be as many perceptions, as many diagrams as there are scholars and observers.

This is my way, and only mine. What I aim to do with this scheme is to simplify the complexity, convey how I felt and interpret that place I reached, where I felt my Expanded

Consciousness, united with Everything (something that may even change in a future experience).

And what I feel is that I was in that Zone 2. I suppose that the one who dies reaches Zone 3. And I repeat: who knows what lies beyond! I do know that from Zone 2, one feels the vast consciousness, swollen, like an infinite balloon of energy; a beautiful sensation vibrating at the highest level of our Being.

But I return to the present moment of my experience.

Healing the Body

Suspended Being, mind and heart in this expansive sensation, I feel overflowing with knowledge; it's a sensation that could be of arrogance, and yet it's one of infinite humility instead. It's as if I don't deserve to know so much, as if being (and having been) in such a sacred place were too much of a privilege. Perhaps, when one transcends arrogance, there is only gratitude.

Suddenly, I am back in my body, on the thin mat. The trance, however, continues. I still feel the Expanded Consciousness; a bit less, but expanded nonetheless.

I think: *There must still be hours of this ceremony left. I have to take advantage of the contact with this energy, with this power... Utilize it for something.*

And I begin to use my hands. As if from them emanates the gentle warmth of that spring of love and wisdom, I place them in different parts of my body. I start with the heart and stomach. I move on to the forehead and throat. I try to traverse the areas of my chakras, although I don't have precise knowledge of where they are and what they are. Then, I place my palms on my lower back (which usually bother me) and continue, pausing for long minutes in each area of my physical body.

It must have been five or seven hours since the first dose.

The dew of the plant is subsiding in my body. Something, perhaps my mind, insists that if I have been in contact with that higher energy, I have to take advantage of its luminous healing beam... But it's more of a desire than a thought.

Healing the Tree

As the areas of my body that needed healing come to an end, I continue squeezing what remains of this Supreme Force and try to send this Light to my family tree.

Even if it's not what was expected, I begin with my aunt Ana, perhaps because she was the one who initiated me into this endless journey of personal growth.

I continue with my father, my sister, and all the paternal ancestors. With my head turned to the left, as if they were all on that side, I share this power with them.

Then, I turn to my right and do the same with the maternal branch. In this state of happiness, I imagine everyone, from my mother backward, also happy, smiling, receiving through me the will of the Higher Consciousness. Next, I do it with my wife, Susana, and with her own family of origin: my brothers-in-law, my in-laws, my nephews...

Each of these moments is slow and enduring. And even though I have nothing to measure time, I know there is still a lot of the ceremony left. There is no rush within me. Everything is present. I remember something I read once: "If you asked a plant what time it is, it would answer you: 'Now.'" With that sensation, I decide to give myself energy, radiate it within me.

My touch is now on my back. Each side receives its own root; one the maternal strength, while the other receives the paternal. Both propel me forward. I stay in that position for a very, very long time...

Still lying down, with my arms above my shoulders and palms open on my shoulder blades, in a position that in a yoga class I wouldn't have endured for more than two minutes, the gentle sap of my ancestors flows into my body, strengthening my Being.

That Voice, again

Ever since I returned from that place where I felt the Expanded Consciousness, I feel, I cannot deny it, the desire to return to it, and again the contradictory thought: *That's it, I can't claim to return there. I've already been, I've seen, I've learned what I needed to learn from that place. I shouldn't abuse it.* And yet I know that we all deserve it because it's the place we belong to!

What I feel is a deep respect that tells me not to abuse it. And I think this every time I want to go back. So, I accept it. *No, I won't search for that tunnel again; it's fine, I have received what I had to receive. Now, I am going to focus on healing my body and using this energy for other things.* And at some point, while (or by) accepting this... boom!

I start ascending again, through a similar but even straighter tunnel, upwards. It's a shortcut; it will take even less time to reach that Origin of all things. And as I travel through the steep cosmic tube, I ask in astonishment: "But... can I go back now?"

A voice, as if joking, responds: "Yes, but be aware that this time I'm going to take you very far."

It's the same Voice –I will realize later– as that shark which, swimming alongside me in the midst of that emerald sea, had said with a certain mischief: "Why would I eat you if I'm not hungry?"

In that identical tone, now ascending back to that place of total expansion, these words ring out: "But mind you, this time I'm going to take you very far." They sound like a warning, both dangerous and amusing at the same time.

Very far, I think, and interpret that it would be like moving to "Zone 3"; in other words, dying! Yet, for some strange reason, I feel no fear. The voice is very familiar, friendly. Its tone is playful.

As all these thoughts come and go, my Being continues to ascend through the tunnel, and finally, I arrive, for the second time, in the cosmic place.

As in the first time, the sensation of Expanded Mind is indescribably beautiful. But, more importantly, I now recognize something that becomes evident to me: the voice sounds exactly... like me.

The voice is none other than myself. I am speaking to myself. I am doing it just like in those moments when, without tension, I simply express myself playfully, jokingly, naturally. And I understand it clearly...

That is the voice of my Higher Consciousness, my Wise Inner Self.

I also realize that, in my life, that's the voice I must listen to. Because it is also true that, more often than I would like, there is another voice within me. It is the one that, after a mistake, punishes me, the one that says, "You're an idiot." Or: "It's unacceptable to waste that time," when maybe I've just missed a highway exit. That voice is the one that judges me all the time for not being "perfect"; that is the voice I shouldn't listen to.

On the other hand, this Voice, calm, wise, the one that hints affectionately, "Don't be afraid, I'm a friendly shark," or "Mind you, if we overshoot from there, you might go too far," is the true Voice, the one of my Wise Inner Self.

Here is an important lesson from my experience. I must learn to recognize the voice of my Higher Consciousness, listen to it more, let it sound more in my life; seek it when I need it, to heed its guidance.

The sadness of humanity

I estimate that there should be around an hour of the ceremony left, and I no longer know how to make the most of this connection, this experience. I'm only aware of enjoying it a lot. *How is it possible to be connected with the Source and not have experienced any fear, I wonder. How can it be that I haven't seen the feared dragon, that I haven't suffered that "death in life" they talk about?* As soon as this thought finishes, it merges with a profound sadness; one that grows rapidly inside me; a sadness that I suddenly realize is not mine. And as if my feelings were anticipating actual events, the music playing in the speakers starts changing its mood, becoming gently sad.

Just as, moments before, the greenish-blue drops were born from the molecules of the music to merge into an ocean, now those notes are dull, blackish. I notice that, from my left, where the low notes flow, a bunch of souls is passing over my body, towards my right. They are sorrowful souls resembling gray ghosts, with hollow, deep, elongated eyes, with open mouths, as in Munch's painting "The Scream." And before my closed eyes... the sadness of Humanity passes.

Mass graves pass... executions, hunger, injustice, torture; the ceaseless pain that comes from our origin.

Rivers of tears once again flow, silently but constantly, into my ears. The tears are mine, but they are not personal. Despite the empathy that such deep sorrow causes in my heart, I do not feel it within me. What I feel is something I have never experienced on such a scale. It is an enormous compassion, so great that I never imagined.

It reminds me of Holocaust movies.

In those images, one usually projects oneself, feels the sadness, and cries. But this time, I *observe* those souls, see their sorrow, and feel profound compassion. It's as if I'm flying with them, saying, "I'm here," "I see you," "how can I help you?" "I'm with you." And yes, tears come out. But they are of pity, not of grief.

Finally...gratitude

I begin to feel that the plant is reaching the end of its work. "Grandmother" has shown me much more than I expected. When I took the ayahuasca, I had said, as recommended: "Show me what I need to see, show it to me with Love," an invocation to which I added (partly out of fear, partly out of caution): "... up to the point that is healthy for me."

As I started to relax, I had done so with some fear. I was trying to control my mind from wandering too much, making it difficult for the plant to take effect on me.

In that mantra "I Surrender, I Trust, I Accept, and I am Grateful," there was a hint of panic, as if I were saying, "I surrender, okay, I did it. I trust this shaman, or at least I want to. I accept whatever comes, but please, let there be no psychotic episode... And whatever happens will be fine, I'll be grateful for it."

Despite my body and mind relaxing like never before thanks to the plant, I, my ego, still wanted to control the situation; with the mantra or whatever it took. So now, at the end of this experience, I remember those words of fearful commitment.

From this present moment, I thank the plant; everyone here, in the room, living their own journey; that voice of the shark, my Higher Consciousness. And I feel a strong urge to go out and write down everything I've experienced, so as not to forget it. *If I don't do it now* –I tell myself–, *will these incredible insights that have come to my consciousness fade away too soon?* Yet, for now, I remain lying down, still. I listen to the last notes of the shamanic music, with my eyes closed. I savor this experience in the deep greenish-blue sea of my Being.

LESSONS FROM THE FIRST EXPERIENCE

In the days that followed, as I reviewed what I had experienced during that ceremony, I began to recognize transformative situations. The main ones were these, in order of appearance; but always in quantum dialogue with each other:

1) **That place exists**. I call "place" a state; that of having felt Expanded Consciousness. More than a physical location, it was a complete experience that offered me a broader perspective on life. That place exists; it's where we come from, where I will go, and where my deceased relatives are. When a loved one dies, I will know that they will be experiencing that state. Consequently, even if my ego mourns, my soul can be at peace. This is something I always "knew," albeit at an intuitive-rational level. Since adolescence, I told myself, "When someone dies, we cry out of selfishness, not because that person is doing badly or suffering from death. That person is fine (or at least we cannot claim they are suffering)." But now I have truly *experienced* that sensation, that place, that state. The conviction is now internal, rooted in the spiritual realm.

2) **I can heal!** From that spiritual plane experience, unintentionally, I began to transfer it to the psychological and everyday plane. I usually have a persistent fear in my

life. It's small but constant. Even when I open emails, I feel an imminent threat, fearing to encounter disastrous news, the announcement that I will lose everything. I know that this fear is not rational, and there is no probable risk. But it's there, underlying, subjugating. And when a more significant situation for me arises (such as recently, when buying a car), that fear suddenly magnifies. I have identified where it comes from, but it remains distressing. It's like having a fear of heights and finding oneself at the edge of a precipice.

My therapist, Mauricio, told me that when I feel this (opening emails, etc.), take a second, "put a chair" in front of me, sit my wounded inner child in it, and ask him, "What's going on with you?" Instead of trying to solve what troubles him, just listen attentively, understand, and feel.

That's what I did, for example, when returning from buying the car, every time I felt discomfort, when checking emails... And it worked!

For the first time in my life, I could connect with my fear, rather than understanding it intellectually or emotionally. Until now, my thirty-something years of therapy and personal work have been spent analyzing, covering the problem from a thousand different angles, and exploring dozens of techniques: Family Constellations, visualization, hypnosis, meditation, etc. As a result, I understand my neurosis and its origin in detail. But I had never thought, let alone proven, that I can **connect** with the problem!

Being in that state of Expansion was a genuine awareness: I *knew* that place existed, but... "*Being* there?" "Can I really experience that?"

Yes, and so it was. I realized that it's not just something I believe exists, and others can experience. From that spiritual plane, I could see that I can connect with my inner child. For the first time in my life, I realized, became aware that healing is possible. I had always thought that through therapy, someday, it was likely that I would feel better. And so it has been, of course. But now I positively believe that I deserve, I can heal; to stop feeling that fear, that cloud that has hovered over me since childhood. And consequently...

3) **Fear can "disappear."** We only need to look at it instead of escaping from it or trying to resolve it. I now think about that friendly shark that accompanied me underwater, then of that black hole I was trying not to face directly. I realize that these were "representations of my fears." I understand that by facing them head-on, accepting them, letting them in, surrendering to them, they cease to be dangerous. On the contrary, they become passageways to the next level.

The shark, which was nothing less than the Voice of my Wise Inner Self, came with its mouth open, and it didn't bite me! But instead of recognizing it, I doubted. I asked, over and over, mistrusting my own wisdom, if it was going to eat me. And finally, when I understood that it wouldn't bite me, the tunnel came, taking me upwards to the next experience.

Later, I felt that black hole on my left side, the "Here comes fear, the dragon." Yet, when I turned my head and let it in, the other tunnel came, the even faster route to the place of total Expanded Consciousness. It was a beautiful lesson. When fear comes, I must stop and, instead of "resolving" (which is what I always do), I just need to look at it, "breathe it in," and accept whatever comes. That's precisely what I have been doing since the weeks following the ceremony. When I'm about to open an email, I stop, close my eyes, and ask the child inside me what's going on. I simply listen, without trying to provide solutions or explain anything. The anxiety, the anguish doesn't completely vanish, but they lessen.

4) **That is the Voice of my Higher Self.** I have learned to recognize that Voice in my everyday life, to become aware of it, to differentiate its sound from the voices of my ego, and

to summon it whenever I want. The kind attitude of the shark (my Wise Inner Self) has expanded further over time. Its influence is not limited to significant life moments but extends to simple and everyday ones.

One day, for example, I was at the gym, and after finishing my aerobic routine, I felt like going swimming. But I also wanted to go home to rest. So, in the locker room, I looked at myself in the mirror and thought: *What would the shark's voice say now?* And it said: "Come on, don't you love swimming and relaxing in the water?" So I made the effort, put on my swimsuit, showered, and got into the pool. I swam just four laps and told myself: *Well, that's it; this is actually more than what I was planning to do.* And immediately: *I'll do one last slow lap, like in slow motion, as if resting or meditating.* As soon as I did so, I started to feel an incredible sense of relaxation and pleasure, as if it were an orgasm for the soul. Simply by swimming slowly, in slow motion! I thought: *Wow, the sensations one can create in their body and mind just by making a slow movement!* It was revealing. And that had arisen just by listening to my Wise Inner Self, the voice of my friendly shark.

PART II

*A Family Constellation in the Universe
The Connection with Others*

SECOND INTAKE OF AYAHUASCA

JUNE 11 AND 12, 2021

The magic exists. What was once magic is now... science. Much of what seems impossible or even absurd to us today is something we still cannot explain through reason. Just as there were tasks performed by a sorcerer in the past, now handled by an MRI or other computerized machine, connections currently limited to magical realms will become scientific axioms tomorrow. After traversing a night in the very Hell, in this second ceremony, I accessed that science of the future, those ties that bind us humans like invisible threads, akin to those connecting the stars.

A deeper understanding of "magic"

In my first experience with the Amazonian substance, the journey had been deep into my *interior* and from there to that place where Consciousness is truly Expanded and merges with the universe. In the second, the main connection was with my *exterior*, that inner part connected to everything around us.

Let's make a brief imaginary parenthesis here to provide context for what follows. Once, visiting the Griffith Observatory in Hollywood, California, I had a thought that, like a coin dropping into a video game machine, activated old knowledge and clarified a very simple fact about the origins of the universe. In the museum on the ground floor hangs a giant Periodic Table of Elements. If you press a button, the three basic elements that emerged from the Big Bang light up: lithium, hydrogen, and helium. Everything else originated from them.

Risking a very simplistic theory of the beginnings of the world (other components were added, mixed, and evolved), we could say that everyone and everything, from a stone to a brain cell, observed with a powerful enough magnifying glass, would reveal that we are made of the same stuff! Isn't this an incredibly marvelous concept?

But now, let's think about it in reverse (and again, I warn that this is not a proven scientific theory but rather a personal reasoning based on the scientific method).

The first digital computer in history, known as ENIAC and built in the 1940s, had titanic dimensions (occupying an area of 1743 sq. ft., with a total weight of 27 tons) and had memory just enough to perform basic calculations. Forty years later, the first personal computer with which this author had contact, the Commodore 64, only had a memory of 64 bytes, which would be exhausted today with the words on this page! Needless to say, in the present, tens of terabytes fit on the tip of a finger, and it doesn't make much sense to do calculations at this point because it's no longer a matter of space.

By simple logic, as technology continues to evolve, there will come a time (if it hasn't already) when the physical storage of information will shrink more and more until it becomes not only invisible but ethereal.

What is information traveling through Bluetooth, WiFi, or other intangible means if not this?

And thinking even further, won't thoughts, the human soul, be pure bytes of information? Therefore, it is not ridiculous to think about telepathy or a person with such high sensitivity that they can read another's unconscious, even if it sounds like "magic" today.

Probably, centuries ago, an enlightened person could feel that someone had an organ problem by just laying hands on them. In our time, such a sorcerer would have lost their job in favor of a simple imaging diagnostic device. And while many, past and present, were mistaken (or consciously deceived) in readings of the unknown, there still exist those few, select, and hyper-perceptive individuals who can interpret, almost mathematically, the signs of the stars or read the signals of our unconscious.

It's almost not about believing in their existence anymore but about finding that "one in a million," discoverable in the crowded ranks of modern wizards (astrologers, psychics, etc.); that chosen one who, due to their high level of vibration, approaches the accuracy of a "computed tomography" of the future. However, it's likely that this "magic" can only provide *general* clues to that exact science that still remains hidden, rather than delving into the details. Thus, the modern numerologist may be right in saying, for instance, "The problem is in your liver." And we immediately want to know, "So, should I have surgery on the seventh or eighth day?" The responsible answer, for now, would be: "To be precise, we should wait fifty or a hundred years until a scientific device appears that can give us the exact answer."

The same applies to ayahuasca. It provides access to that magic. And, in the same way, we shouldn't demand more from it than general answers or try to use it to explain every detail or generalize our personal experiences.

Most of these "wizards" (the genuine ones) don't even need ayahuasca to express their gifts. But perhaps, with sufficient preparation and the right purpose, an ordinary person like the one writing these lines, with the help of some master plant, can access similar understandings for a few moments; even understand that very connection that exists between all things, people, and the universe all which, in the end, are composed of the same basic elements, just vibrating at different frequencies.

In any case, facing the possibility of accessing these encrypted truths, it is important to do so consciously. And while it is true that God lives in us, that God is the energy vibrating in every molecule, and therefore, "I am God," we must be aware of our "divine limitations." As some wise man said: "I don't know who God is, but at least I know that I am not Him." In other words: balance, always balance.

The truth is that everything is invisible matter, and everything invisible, in the correct frequency, can materialize. Everything is information, energy. Someday we will understand this definitively, and we will read it in a science manual.

Meanwhile, there are people with a certain degree of evolution in some aspect of their being. They can control at least that aspect of their energy, those vibrations. They can materialize magic, the kind that ayahuasca also allow us tap into.

But before falling into the common trap of trying to explain what is still unexplainable, let's close this parenthesis and return to Earth. Let's not disconnect too much because we are about to delve into a beautiful experience.

We are all addicts

As expressed in the Introduction, in the first ceremony, I had found within myself a deep understanding that drugs are neither good nor bad but merely tools, neutral tools. Everything depends on the purpose for which they are used (the true and profound purpose, not the one deceiving our minds). Thus, addictions, whose purpose is to numb pain, *dis-connect* us from life. In contrast, based on what I have learned and as long as it is used with spaced frequency, ayahuasca produces the opposite effect: it *connects* us with the life force, the Source.

And it is important here to address the issue of addictions not only on a personal level. We often think of them solely in connection with drugs. However, there are dozens of addictions: to sex, tobacco, alcohol, social media, video games, television, and a long etc. Some are less obvious than others, especially those linked to a "value" or something socially considered "good," such as work or study. Our common logic tells us that if "work" is good, excessive work is very good. But here, Aristotelian reasoning does not apply. Work is an addiction that many use, as always, to escape from something painful, like being at home with their family. Another type of addiction associated with a positive value has accompanied me since I can remember. It has been present for many years in my personal struggles, and it is the addiction to food or overeating.

Whether associated with a value or an obvious lack of value, for the purpose of this work, all addictions are equal: their goal is to escape from pain. This must be clear if we want to progress in self-awareness. All typical excuses ("everyone has to die of something," "I only smoke two cigarettes a day," "I'm a *connoisseur*," etc.) are nothing but the voice of our addictive mind. No one, from their true Inner Self, wants to depend on a substance or activity that controls them or, worse yet, causes problems in their life. However, almost everyone suffers from one addiction or another.

And thus, in the pure sense that an addiction is a repetitive action of our mind that "binds" us and subjects us to something that, in our sound judgment, we would prefer not to do, we are all addicts.

One more clue...

I suggest thinking about the ayahuasca experience as a clue in the "video game" of life. As Manuel, the numerologist, expressed in our meeting, let's imagine for a moment that we are all Beings of Pure Consciousness (our own Higher Selves). We all inhabit that Zone 3 in the Space plane I referred to in Part I. Suddenly, perhaps "bored" with Eternal Peace, we want to experience the material, relive pain, remember how roasted meat tastes (with my apologies to vegetarians). So, we look towards the immense video game that is Earth and decide to descend to play. We choose an avatar that, along with its genuine identity, will enjoy certain powers (talents) and weaknesses (physical or mental illnesses, traumas), simple tools that we decide to take to make the game interesting. Some, tired of being the Brad Pitt of the game, choose to be disabled or chronically ill.

We enter the first screen (or perhaps the level we exited in the previous life) knowing that it's just a game, right? Because, win or lose, if the game ends soon, we will return to the "boredom" of Painless Eternity. But we also hope that, entered into a certain level or "screen" of the game, we can exit it in some *higher* phase. Perhaps it's a match that lasts an indefinite amount of time and space (at least indefinite for the human mind).

And so, we play. And like in any game, from time to time, under a rock or behind a painting, we find a clue that gives us special knowledge or helps us advance a little faster.

Well, I see ayahuasca as that clue in the game of life. Like a momentary zoom-out that elevates us on the path and shows us where we are located on the map of this screen.

However, as revealing as the experience may be, if we were to take ayahuasca very frequently, even with the manifest purpose of *connecting*, we would actually be seeking to *disconnect* from the game, trying to return to the Eternity and Expanded Mind of our Higher Selves too quickly. It would be like a kind of "addiction to Knowledge" when, in reality, we already know that "I only know that I know nothing." And on the other hand, what fun would a video game be with lots of clues on every screen, at every step, in every level? Who would want to play Pac-Man if every screen were filled with magical pills, those that kill the ghosts? We would get bored soon! It would be better not to play.

Therefore, if *disconnecting* too much is addiction to escape from pain, is it permissible to *connect* too much? Exactly, it is, once again, the old concept of balance, which must be applied to everything; a concept that is precisely on the opposite side of addictions. So, as explained above, ayahuasca is a drug less prone to addiction since it connects us with pain instead of disconnecting us. And returning to the clue itself, no matter how sporadic it is, it won't make much sense if we don't know our avatar's capabilities in-depth. That is, without a framework of personal development and deep knowledge of our Self and our psychology (essentially two points on the same invisible line), the clue cannot be interpreted or genuinely utilized. It would be like getting a strange and powerful shield on some screen but not knowing how or when to put it on the avatar: it will look nice and fit well, but it will lack any utility.

Thus, these types of occurrences beyond ordinary experience are like opening wide a door to the unconscious; but also to other levels, intensely connected with this one: the Expanded Consciousness of the Universe, as I felt it in my first ayahuasca ceremony in Madrid; the collective unconscious (Carl Jung) or the morphogenetic field of our ancestors (Bert Hellinger).

About this last point, the great discovery of Hellinger, creator of Family Constellations, was the experience that I will narrate in the next pages.

It was a connection not only with my Inner Wise Self and Expanded Mind (as in my first ceremony) but between these and the almost thirty "strangers" with whom I shared this second ceremony. An invisible bond was formed with all those people. They, in an astonishing way, represented facets of my personality and my life, including my own addiction. It was something magical but full of common sense. After all, like branches of the same tree, the stories and traumas are all the same, sharing the same origin: our roots as humanity.

A framework of psychological understanding

The previous experience, a year and a half before this one, had been an internal journey from my fears to that place where we all come from and where we all go. In contrast, if I could title this second intake (something impossible to summarize in words), it would be that of a "Great Session of Family Constellations," with all the resources of the universe as a stage and in service of my healing.

During the ayahuasca experience, consciousness is not lost, and the mind does not dissolve. One lives and analyzes simultaneously what is happening. Or at least, that's what happens to me, thanks to decades of work on myself. Therefore, before delving into the experience itself, I would like to share the "intentions" that occupy my personal work these days. Not out of excessive egocentrism, but because they will serve as a framework for understanding what happened in this second ceremony.

In my current process of "Matrix Scenes", an innovative approach created by Argentinean therapist Mauricio Weintraub, I have concluded that my main themes are as follows:

- **Structure**: a "violent mother" (yet overprotective) and an "absent father" (one who remained silent and did not defend me against my mother's madness and who did not support me in crucial moments of my life).
- **Symptoms**: as I mentioned before, I am addicted to food, compulsively. Additionally, I often act as if "everyone wants to attack me"; I have an issue with money (saving or investing out of fear of a supposed "catastrophe," which exists only in my mind), and

some other minor mechanisms that we create to numb the pain.
- **Paradigm shift**: perhaps it is that life structure that led me to always act under an imperative: "fight, fight, fight." Thanks to this attitude (I must admit), I have achieved a prosperous and quite happy life. I have developed in a job that I am passionate about and that allows me to live comfortably, so I am immensely grateful. However, that paradigm of perpetual combat, driven by "fear of catastrophe," has its cost. It consumes much of my energy (compulsively saving, excessive planning, self-imposing, etc.) and prevents me from moving to the "next level" in my life. Therefore, my current goal is to achieve a paradigm shift; allow myself to lose, accept that there may be things in life that I don't like, pay the costs of it without complaining, tolerate that people think differently than I do...
- **Setting new goals**: in the video game allegory, I feel suspended, unable to "move to the next level." I am trying to discover what is next for me; that is my challenge for the future. Once I have succeeded in everything I set out to do so far (building a family, achieving a successful career, economic security, a company that gives me much joy), I wonder: What is it that I really like? What does my inner child want to play?

I list these elements again because they are relevant to understanding the process that ayahuasca produced in me. When one faces the decision to take this ancestral "medicine," one usually does so with certain "intentions" about what they want to work on. My list had to do with the four mentioned keys. Hopefully, the reader can capitalize on my experience as a benchmark for their possible personal one.

During those days, I also had a strong pain in the lower back, and I wrote in my journal something that occurred to me at that moment: "What does my back pain mean? Perhaps that I am not entirely upright in my actions?" So, I threw my questions out to the universe; I surrendered them.

However, I am very cautious (or fearful?) about drugs, and I had internalized that "no matter how specific you ask the plant for something, it will teach you what you need at that moment... and nothing more or less." So, I tried to approach this sacred medicine without specific expectations. Once again, my wish in front of it was: "Show me what I need to know at this moment, and to the extent that is healthy for me."

Then, when taking it, I repeated the mantra "I Surrender, I Trust, I Accept, and I am Grateful." This, I recall, was equivalent to: "I surrender to this experience, trust the shaman and all those who are here, accept whatever comes, and thank for whatever happens, be it what it may."

Once again, I realize that this sounds very good and reflects the most genuine and respectful way to surrender to the master plant. But I also recognize that a little bit of that "fear" of something "bad" happening creeps into it.

And before submerging into the experience itself, I would like to mention two things that happened to me in the days leading up to it, and that gained subsequent meaning.

Take me

In my therapy session two days before the ceremony, I hesitated to mention to Mauricio, my psychologist, that I was going to take ayahuasca. I understood that he wasn't a "fan" of that path, and I feared that what he might say could influence my experience. So, I started that session with him trying to cover another topic during the usual fifty minutes or so.

But as we talked about that necessary "paradigm shift," Mauricio told me that my problem is that I argue against his proposals, and that the argument is another tool in my "fight, fight, fight" mode. Then, in a completely "casual" manner, he said, "You don't *take* me, you have to *take* me, Gerardo. Take me, take what I tell you, trust me and take me, without arguing, without fighting, and you will be able to progress faster."

Of course, I, who didn't want to tell him that I was going to "take" ayahuasca, couldn't avoid the topic any longer and said, "Well, now that you talk about *taking* you, I feel like I have to confess something: I didn't want to tell you that this Saturday I am taking ayahuasca for the second time."

It was a humorous "coincidence." He said it was okay, that it wasn't his path, and that in any case, he didn't judge me. He did feel, however, "jealous" that I could take ayahuasca and surrender, and couldn't surrender and trust his proposal without always arguing.

That was the end of the session. But Mauricio appeared in the ayahuasca... and boy... I took him. Of course, I took him.

Night premonition?

Another significant anecdote from the week before the ceremony was a dream.

I was in the ceremony, with the shaman and all the participants standing, forming a circle. Ivan (whom I only knew by phone until then) placed little papers at the feet of each one. When I read the one that corresponded to me from above, I saw the word 'Satan' written on it. Even within the dream, I was terrified. I tried to move the paper with my foot, surreptitiously, without anyone noticing it, to place it on the spot of the participant next to me.

It's funny now that I tell it, but that nocturnal vision caused me considerable fear. It was as if the dream was telling me, 'In ayahuasca, you will encounter Satan!'

I remember wanting to forget that dream that night. The truth is that, by the day of the ceremony, I didn't remember it at all... until I found myself in the middle of Hell.

A double bet

After that first experience in the Sierra de Madrid, I thought all ceremonies would be more or less the same in their dynamics. But they are not.

At a friend's house in Los Angeles, I had met a girl who talked about a group with which she had recently taken ayahuasca. Ivan, the shaman she mentioned, happened to be from my hometown. The Argentine community in Los Angeles is not very large. Generally, if we don't know each other, we have at most one degree of separation from others. But I had never heard of this Ivan guy.

I contacted him first by text, and then we briefly spoke on the phone. He seemed very pleasant and instilled confidence in me, despite my natural caution and the prejudice many of us have with our own people.

When Ivan sent me information about his ceremony, which would be in June, at a residence in the mythical city of Topanga Canyon, I set out to review the program carefully.

His communication said:

Hello everyone! The day of the next ceremony has arrived. We welcome you to our new temple, which has an immense ceremony room and an acre and a half of park with incredible views of Topanga Canyon's mountain. You can leave the city and feel like you are entering a retreat in nature, just minutes from LA. We invite you to this life-changing experience. We will provide you with foam mattresses, buckets (for vomiting), water, blankets, cushions, a professional menu from our chef Nicole, and everything you need. The idea is for you to feel welcome from your arrival at our space.

Following this, there was the schedule of activities:

Friday, June 11
12:00: Start fasting.
16:30: Arrival; find your place.
18:00: Introduction.
19:30: Central Piece - Night session; begins with 'Mother' (another name given to ayahuasca, avoiding mentioning it in the email).

Saturday, June 12

07:00: Central Piece - In the morning, we start with 'Father' (code name for the ancient cactus called San Pedrito).
13:30: Meditation and sound bath - Gong / Hang Drum.
14:30: Lunch prepared by our incredible chef.
15:00: Circle to share experiences.
16:30: Rest until the second ceremony of the night.

And the outline repeated, with some variations, the next day.

The proposal of this new shaman involved not one, but four doses! Two full days of ayahuasca and San Pedrito. Four drugs!

My prejudice and concern increased; the plant offered to double the bet, and I knew I shouldn't resist ("Drugs are neither good nor bad; everything depends on the purpose...". My own words now echoed in my mind).

The adult in me began to investigate what this San Pedrito, called 'Father,' was.

In our previous conversation, Ivan clarified that this plant has a very mild effect, almost like that of a relaxant, and its goal is to extend the "exit" effect of ayahuasca; to stretch its last hours when only sensitivity and reflection remain, with consciousness and common sense awake. The goal would then be to prolong a meditation for hours, to internalize everything learned during the night. Anyway, that sounded like an excess, a madness to me.

In the first experience, which was more of a journey into my interior, the "integration" of everything learned manifested itself in the days after the ceremony. That's why it seemed natural to summarize it in the section "Lessons from the First Experience", pages ago.

However, in this second opportunity, which lasted more than twenty-four hours, the "Profound Understandings" (as I will call them) were happening in the ceremony itself, mostly during the morning and the following afternoon. Therefore, instead of placing them as the final conclusion of the chapter, I will integrate them into the experience, in the more or less exact order in which they were "exploding" in that continuous present.

A house on the hill

As suggested by Ivan's schedule, I started my fast at noon. Additionally, I had avoided the unnecessary ingestion of animal meat during the preceding days, as far as my addiction allowed. I also made an effort not to take my medications for blood sugar and cholesterol. Although this abstinence wasn't necessary, I wanted to be as detoxified as possible to receive the plant.

Hours later, I was on my way. Since the property had limited parking spaces, I had offered to pick up another participant named Mindy. She was in her thirties and came from some city in the central United States whose name I don't remember. She was a scriptwriter, shy, and kind. This wouldn't be her first experience. Mindy had attended several ceremonies with Ivan, so in the twenty minutes that separated us from our destination, I tried to gather more information from her.

—Ivan is great, —she assured me— Very sweet. He is a shaman who is present for the entire two days. He talks to everyone. Listens and guides everyone.

I wasn't sure if I would muster the courage to do two nights of ayahuasca, so steering the conversation towards what concerned me the most, I asked:

—And... will you stay both nights?

—Of course. Won't you?

Then I honestly expressed my concern and fears.

—Well, don't worry —she responded— Some people stay for only one day. My sister, for example, couldn't do both days, and she'll arrive tomorrow just for the second ceremony.

That reassured me a lot. The shaman had told me over the phone that I could stay only one night, but he hadn't sounded very happy about it. And then I understood why. Ivan, who has officiated more than two hundred ceremonies in his life and is also a chemical engineer, has developed a "formula" of plants (which he cooks himself) and a routine. Both things have taken him a lot of time and dedication, and he is convinced that two days and four doses (two of ayahuasca and two of San Pedrito) are the best way to make the most of the teachings of "Grandmother". With his best intentions, he wants you to experience his "recipe" to the fullest.

As the car moved gently, talking to Mindy helped me assimilate the situation and know that I could choose to stay or not for a second night, without any pressure.

Ascending Old Topanga Canyon's historic road, which connects Calabasas to the Malibu coast, trees begin to cheerfully invade the path. You can feel the change in the air as you leave behind a city polluted by show business, absorbing the "vibes" and colors of the hippie culture of the '60s and '70s. This bohemian enclave is one of the few places in gentrified Los Angeles that has stayed in time. It is still the refuge of musicians, filmmakers, and other artists who, despite living in the mountains, make sure they are twenty minutes from surfing and other sea attractions.

That route, which Robin Williams or Jim Morrison might have taken back to their homes in other times, my new friend and I were traveling, amidst conversations about movies and magic plants. Until, turning right at the corner of a picturesque bar, we zigzagged a little further up the mountain.

The entrance to the property, adorned with a stone arch, reminded me of that first ceremony in the Sierra de Madrid. The car scratched the last stretch of steep dirt, and we arrived at our destination.

We were among the first. At the main door of the spacious house, two immense armchairs rested. Next to them, a few pairs of shoes signaled that I should take off mine. We crossed the door into a room that I already knew from Ivan's email photos. The mattresses were waiting, lying down, for the guests to wake them up from their long nap. There were about thirty spaces with mats, blankets, and cushions. Of course, a small bucket rested next to each of them, with an open mouth.

I crossed the living room. To my left, a bar separated that area from the kitchen. From there, the aroma of an exotic tea reached me. To the right, a large window escaped towards a garden that tumbled down the slender hill. When I was about to go out there, trapped by the landscape, I recognized a familiar voice.

Dressed in white, the young and slim shaman reminded me of myself in some not-so-distant decade.

We hugged and exchanged a few words. I discovered in Ivan a kind, smiling guy, qualities that stood out for his youth. He told me to choose a place and a mattress, and then we would talk with more time. People started arriving with backpacks and barefoot steps.

It took me a while to choose my mat... I first tried one that was close to a speaker. I left my things and lay down on it. From this location, in the middle of the room, I felt too exposed. So, I moved to another environment and tried another one. Here it was too dark, and I couldn't see the shaman's spot.

After trying two or three more, I found one that, right next to a column, offered me the necessary refuge and privacy without making me feel isolated or confined. And I made it my nest.

Again, as in the old Spanish rural house, people exchanged smiles and emitted light sighs, premonitions of deep emotions. Once again, many knew each other. It was my turn to introduce myself to each and every one. This time, I already understood the language of long hugs.

Take one

The introductions were brief. I had hoped to integrate into a group with shared codes, though not with enough confidence to relive common anecdotes. A Russian woman in her fifties, who asserted herself despite her small stature, introduced her daughter, even thinner than her. Behind them, a bulky Brazilian, tanned and with such perfect muscles that he could have doubled for "The Incredible Hulk," shook my hand kindly.

From the other corner of this spiritual ring lined with mats, a friendly chubby man, with whitish skin and a sweaty shirt, smiled delicately at me. I exchanged a few words with him. Upon noticing that I was Argentine, he expressed passion for barbecue. His name was John, and I imagined a more feminine version of "Little John" from Robin Hood.

A beautiful girl with the grace of a Russian dancer warmly greeted everyone except me. In contrast, a plump lady in her fifties, named Barbara, approached me and announced, in a maternal tone, that she would occupy the mat next to mine.

Later, three teenage boys arrived, each on his own. They were all slim and handsome. Justin, agile and outgoing, emanated the energy of someone who romantically embraces every adventure. David, with a thoughtful gaze and an air of perpetual composure, projected a certain intellectual image. Ron, with black skin covering his young muscles and dreadlocks, only lacked Bob Marley's joint. Somehow, I blended them into one person.

Under normal circumstances, in a group where the leader (Ivan) was from Argentina, it would have been natural to encounter other compatriots, or perhaps someone from Spain. However, much to my surprise, most attendees were Russian or American (three or four were African American). Besides the Brazilian, there were no other Latinos. There was a Ukrainian who had come directly from the airport, taking advantage of the trip for other matters in the city.

So, excluding Ivan and partly the Brazilian, no one else spoke my native language or shared a direct or evident root with me. So far, I've exchanged not more than a few words with each of them.

Despite being in the midst of the Covid-19 pandemic, no one wore masks. There was a protocol in place where, out of respect, everyone was required to trust that anyone unvaccinated had a negative test result. However, no one was asked to show such proof.

I remember noticing that the young black man, Ron, had a water bottle exactly like mine. I thought: *I hope I don't mistake his for mine.*

When it was approximately 6:00 PM, as planned, Ivan, leaning against the farthest wall of the room, welcomed us and began his introduction: "Today, I'm accompanied by several helpers. Please, raise your hands, helpers."

Nearly half a dozen hands rose above the heads of the participants.

"I find it incredible. I think I've never been in a ceremony with so many helpers. Thank you all," he continued. And he asked them to say their names so that everyone could identify them. Then he clarified:

Don't think that one or a thousand ayahuasca ceremonies will completely solve a problem or end your suffering. With these experiences, it's about gradually releasing the pain. With each ayahuasca session, the plant gives us more understanding and more peace, and thus, it strips away a little more suffering. But understand that you can't remove it all. You can never completely eliminate sadness. There must always be a little pain —he emphasized on this last concept—. *Otherwise, life would end.*

After explaining the schedule for the day, Ivan mentioned some "guidelines":

While everyone knows that there are no rules in our ceremonies, given our experience, there are certain norms that we will ask you to respect so that we can all have a more productive session.

The first is not to turn on lights. Throughout the night, there will be candles in all areas of the house. No sector is restricted, but please don't turn on the lights because that could distract someone from their journey.

Secondly, we will ask you to give us your mobile phones; we will return them to you tomorrow morning. We don't want anyone to take photos, make calls, recordings, or anything else that could be invasive to the other attendees.

Thirdly, we ask that you don't lock the bathroom from inside. If the door is closed, no one should try to enter, and those inside should know that closing the door is enough. We want to avoid someone reflecting eternally on the toilet and preventing others from using it.

Lastly, you know that during the ceremony, you can scream, make noise, cry, dance, whatever you need. But we ask you to try to avoid spoken words. Not just talking to others but speaking aloud. Why do I say this? Because articulated speech uses a very rational part of the brain, and even if you think you're speaking softly, someone else in the opposite corner of the room may hear it, and it could interrupt their experience.

Ivan continued by indicating that, although everyone came with intentions to heal or work on a specific issue, we should try to become aware of that matter but then let it go. Because, according to him, ayahuasca would lead us only down "the path that our Higher Self knows we must travel today." Therefore, we shouldn't contribute another enigma to the puzzle of our existence.

With that said, the shaman directed his gaze toward me, the only fellow countryman he would see in a long time, and said, "Today, my intention is to work on my roots." I caught that moment, not knowing that this intention, like a dark tomb (as we will later see), would sneak into my ayahuasca reverie.

In his speech, Ivan overcame my initial prejudice despite his apparent youth; this Argentine shaman exuded more wisdom than I had anticipated. And that would help me with the first part of that mantra: "I Surrender, I Trust, I Accept, and I Am Grateful," which was starting to form in my mind.

I took my turn to speak and briefly recounted that in my previous experience in Madrid, I had agreed to take *rapé* (that kind of powdered tobacco that someone blows into your nose with a pipe or horn). I explained that the experience with this powder had been somewhat traumatic, but perhaps it was precisely that shock that had allowed me to enter the wonderful journey of my first ayahuasca.

"I don't want to refuse to ask for *rapé*, –I said–, but I hope I don't need it and that inhaling a bit of the peppermint oil that Mindy offered me will be enough."

Then I added: "If I had to choose an intention for this ceremony, it would be to change a pattern of permanent struggle, one that has stigmatized me since my adolescence..." And briefly explained that "Fight, fight, fight" Paradigm I talked about earlier.

Although I had several topics outlined in my journal, I considered that this was the most important, deserving to be my intention for this second ceremony. Then, like a good student, I let it go. And as I did, my mind whispered another question: "Am I made for transcendent things?" Because it sounded pretentious, grandiose, I immediately dismissed this other underlying intention, not knowing that later it would cost me an enormous battle.

After Ivan's preamble, all participants approached him to take the first shot of ayahuasca. Another one was scheduled fifteen minutes later, from a similar plant whose name I don't remember, a complement to Ivan's recipe.

The surprise was realizing that we would all drink from the same small glass!

In the midst of Covid-19, and despite half being vaccinated and the other allegedly having a negative PCR, putting all lips on the same piece of glass was a challenge. This was particularly potent for me, as I would be the last to drink.

Indeed, the saliva of nearly thirty people mixed with mine. Only later would I realize the true "contagion" because, for the next twenty-four hours, I would be connected through that saliva to each and every one of those twenty-nine beings, in a day of Love, roots, and self-reflections, like I had never experienced before.

Fortunately, not only did I not need the *rapé*, but I didn't even require a second dose of ayahuasca (which one could request an hour after the first dose). Mindy brought me the essential oil, and a few minutes after taking the complementary plant, began what would become, for me, a true anteroom to Hell.

A Concert of Pain

I have already taken the two plants and lie down on my mat. I have my eye mask on, the same one I used the first time in Madrid. Noticing that no one else is covering their eyes, I think that maybe a technique exclusive to that shaman. Nevertheless, I put it on, thinking, "If it worked that time...". Like a good student, I begin reciting my mantra: "I Surrender, I Trust, I Accept, and I am Grateful"...

At that moment, the question I asked myself before comes back to my mind: Does my back pain symbolize that I am not entirely right in my actions? However, I let that thought linger and continue with my mantra: "I Surrender, I Trust, I Accept, and I am Grateful, I Surrender..."

Within a few minutes, before even starting to feel the effects of the plant, two women to my left begin to scream inconsolably, and they just do not stop.

These are not ordinary screams; they are impossible to describe wails of despair. But they don't come from another dimension; these two women are somewhere in the room. One of them (as I will find out later) is Mindy, the timid and pleasant woman I carpooled with on my way here. The screams are the most powerful I have ever heard, desperate cries of pain, with an intensity and volume almost unreal. They echo tirelessly for hours, becoming infinite. They grow *in crescendo*, turning into thunderous cries of pain. Then they huddle, transforming into moans. And as their volume increases again, I feel they are screams of childbirth, of abuse, of centuries of torture endured by all the women throughout history of humanity...

One of them exclaims with anger: "*Get out of my house!*" Even rhythmically: "*Get-out, Get-out*". She doesn't say it just a couple of times; she repeats it more than a hundred times, amidst a tsunami of other cries that flood the place.

The space is no longer the room of a house in the mountains; it's some circle of Dante. And everything that, hidden beneath the eye mask, I hear on my left is met with entirely different screams from one or two men on my right side.

The spasmodic sounds of the boys are like those of a large wolf or a huge bear. Suddenly and spaced, they emit a roar of attack that I think I would be unable to emulate. They are also cries of pain but different. As if suddenly, in the silence on my right side, a ghost in anguish bursts in, howling so loudly that it would frighten even the bravest of mortals.

I take off the sleep mask; the howl of the Bear really scares me. Despite being in a house in Topanga Canyon, with each howl, I feel the ghost rushing towards me. When I uncover my eyes, I don't notice any presence. There is no ghost or bear. There is no movement around me; only mats and people sitting or lying on them. From where the screams come, I see Justin, one of the young men I met upon arrival, rocking himself, hugging his legs. I understand that he must be the one howling. I cover my eyes again.

The screams of the women return to grow, desperate. For hours and hours, they surround me, they don't go away. To my left and right, in the background, a concert of vomiting joins this disharmony. They vomit intensely, as if expelling through their throats their vital organs, all their anger, their fears...

For my part, I add something to this concert of pain. With my mouth open, I emit deep and grave sounds that vibrate like a mantra in the resonant box of my chest.

Even blindfolded, I begin to feel the effect of the plant. My body is numb. My mind, still "aside," remains attentive and conscious but without intervening, without blocking the door open to the depth of my being. My soul floats inches from my chest. And the screams continue, with unprecedented intensity. They surpass even the sensation that would be produced by a horror movie with a seven-speaker surround system. They go on, and on, and on...

In the darkness of my imagination, I glimpse shadows projecting restless ghosts, black and white souls in agony. They shout, vociferate, vomit the pain of centuries, of generations and generations of our ancestors.

The screams of the women, to my sinister, are the blows of abuse by men, of rapes, of burnings at the stakes. They howl in perpetual distress.

The screams of the men, to my dexter, are those of millennia silently enduring forced labor, bearing the weight of sorrow while stifling their voices. They say: "Enough! Enough!" They hoarse their throats. They release the infarct squeezed in the chest. It's the orchestra of a conductor who only wants to concert pain. To make it understood. Seeking to shout it all together, mixed in an omnipresent abyss.

I am in between them. And, inexplicably, I don't feel fear.

Ah... Of course!

Although this ayahuasca journey is so different from the previous one, there is something similar about it. I'm also experiencing profound revelations of knowledge, fundamental understandings, a Deep Understanding, a Wisdom that comes to me in the clearest way I could ever imagine [the screams continue, louder and louder in the background]. But this is a common and ordinary wisdom. It's the kind we all carry within, and now it opens up to my consciousness. And as I exhale, a voice emerges from me saying, "Ah... Of course... Of course."

These words, like in a cinematic fade, blend with the echoes of vomits and the howls of the Bear.

In this place of darkness, I am occasionally overcome by sadness and at times empathy with these declarations of suffering. Never fear.

I wonder: *How is it possible that I don't feel it? I, who sometimes, when stepping into the garage at night, "sense" that something might ambush me from behind in the darkness... How is it possible that now, in the midst of the Ninth Circle of Hell, I am not utterly terrified? Ah... Of course!*

Then the realization emerges:

First Profound Understanding

In Hell, there is no evil. Evil does not exist... Hell is only Pain.

Hell (regardless of what that word means to each one) is filled only with suffering. No one here wants to harm me. They just want me to listen to them, to *see* them. They only demand my attention; they want me to feel their pain.

Moreover, how can there be evil in pain, if many of these cries from women are cries of childbirth, and from the pain of childbirth, life is born? How can pain be bad!

Therefore, there must be a message in it.

Some time ago, I came to the conclusion that people are not bad; that there is no person intrinsically "evil" by nature. There are only people who suffer.

When one suffers, they want to be heard. And it happens that the most common way to be heard is by causing pain to others, so they can see our suffering.

When someone hurts us (with words, with actions of various intensity), what they are saying is, "Don't you realize I'm suffering? Listen to me!" And if we don't listen, they will double down: "I'm going to show you some of my pain so you understand, damn it!" And that's when things can escalate to more unpleasant levels.

And how do I know this? Because I did it.

Seeing the Pain of Others

I remember when, in my adolescence, in high school, along with a group of "bad boys" friends, we mocked a girl who had a prominent nose. We did it by drawing her face with that huge appendage on the blackboard, among other "evil" things. And it pains me to imagine the sorrow we caused that beautiful girl.

Now, in this Purgatory where the cries of these women continue (yes, they continue) like affliction mantras, I can revisit the scene. But I understand that, no matter how apparent the "evil" my friends and I had, in reality, we all suffered a similar pain. Some of us had separated parents; another had lost his mother when he was a toddler; ultimately, we all lived in unstable environments, with absent parents. I'm not trying to justify the sorrow we caused our classmate (or so many others).

I remember that, years later, I apologized to her. She smiled at me, with a gesture of relief, as if she had been waiting for someone to take that dagger out of her chest all that time. We both needed that "I'm sorry."

That pain I inflicted, though it's now at peace, I shall always remember it as a lesson. The one who torments others does so because they suffer inside. It's not about forgiving the aggressor or not, since, in the spiritual realm, nothing is good or bad; there are no victims or victimizers. It's only about being aware of the fact. It's about the *learning* we obtain from it.

And although, to the right and left, the screams in this room flood my present, it is this profound understanding that waters my journey with peace.

Immersed in a small pause, in a crack of calm, I seek to continue my own path. I believe that if I turn my head forward, I can once again experience that beautiful tunnel, which I carry imprinted in my memory from the ceremony in Madrid. I want to ascend, once again, to that place of Expanded Consciousness and see what the master plant has to teach me in this new experience.

But I can't. The tearing of these throats won't leave me in peace. It's as if the women on my left are pulling down my shirt: "Look at me! Listen to my pain!" And as if from my right, the pain of the Man who doesn't scream desperately but "suffers in silence," who endures the pain, suddenly exploded with a violent scream, grabbing my arm with both hands to prevent me from turning my gaze forward.

Neither of them allows me to continue my path. At least, not until I decide to listen to them.

The truth is that people harm us, and we harm them. This does not mean that we will allow someone to harm us just because we are "aware" of their pain. We should not tolerate or justify harm. It's more about *understanding* the supposed perpetrator. It's even possible that, if one could show them that we see and hear their pain, they would stop.

It is clear that we would not achieve this in all situations. If someone comes to rob us or kill us, it is likely that, no matter how much we try to say "I hear you, I see your pain," we may not be able to make them cease their attempt.

Even so, at this moment, a thought comes to me:

> ### Second Profound Understanding
>
> ***If we see the pain of those who harm us, they may no longer need to harm us.***
>
> If we approach the issue of "evil" from this perspective of love; if we understand that those who come to torment us are actually screaming for us to listen to them, it is very likely that we can reduce or perhaps even avoid their aggressiveness towards us and an imminent harm.
>
> Only circumstances and the level of wisdom and evolution of each of us can determine the outcome. But I invite the reader, the next time they face someone who wants to harm them, and if the situation allows, to think to themselves, as if telling the other person: "I see your suffering."

And I heard the pain of The Woman

Lying on the mat, always aware of everything happening within and around me, I understand that if I want to continue my own journey, I must first listen to the pain of these women who continue with their screams. I know that, in some way, they externalize the pain I hold; they scream for me.

It's difficult for me not to judge them, just as not judging myself is challenging. I must let them know that I see them, hear them. But wait! I recall that in the introductory talk, the shaman told us that one of the rules was not to use spoken words because it could bring someone back from their essential state to intellect.

I don't want to interrupt anyone's journey, but I want to tell these women: "I see you, I hear you; I feel your pain." They need to hear that as much as I need to continue my own path. But how to do it without words?

Amidst these piercing screams that drill through the hours, I turn my head to the left. And with my eyes covered, I see the pain of the Woman, and I say to them: "I see you, I hear you; I hear your pain. It's OK". I do it first in their language, then in Spanish: "*Las veo, las escucho; escucho vuestro dolor. Todo está bien.*" I say it very softly, knowing that they somehow hear me. I'm not sure if I want to calm them with paternal words. I don't know if, terrified, I want to silence that echo pounding in my ears.

Then, in that space to my left, I not only see the pain of the Woman. I see myself in my adolescence, in those blurry moments when I cried inconsolably, shouting with all my strength: "Why, why, why do I have to suffer so much! I don't deserve this. I want to stop suffering." In those moments, tortured by my mother's words or beatings, I cried uncontrollable tears. And with red eyes and a swollen face, I repeated to myself: "I want to die. I want God to come down and kill me. I know suicide isn't right, so please, God, end my life, end this suffering, I can't take it anymore..." The women's screams in this room (I can almost feel the pain in their throats) echo those of my mother. I want to see their pain. But I only see mine.

They don't stop screaming. I've done voice work in film sessions, where I had to scream for a couple of hours, but spaced out; maybe about twenty minutes in total. I remember suffering chest and throat pain even for a whole week afterward. How can these two women humanly scream so much and for so many hours without interruption? If those screams don't shred their throats, they peel my heart.

The screams not only disrupt others' journeys; they unbalance the energy in the environment. Through the sounds around me, I decipher the movements, the restlessness of others, how the helpers try to control the situation. One assistant is singing *ikaros* (rhythmic sacred songs); two others are playing indigenous instruments. They try to use music to drown out the screams to my left. They gradually lower they voices and decelerate their chants so that the two women (because there are only two) catch the descending movement. Perhaps, at the same time, they are soothing them (the screams surely reach neighboring homes). I envision in my mind how the shamans surround the two women and lead them, with the rhythm of the song, toward a supposed "end," softening it so that they blend with this decreasing motion. Other assistants join the arduous task. Several assistants and healers armed with maracas, flutes, rattles, and small drums are needed to pacify the spirits of pain.

And slowly, with the slowing down of the shamanic music, the women's screams turn into spaced gasps. This lasts only a few seconds. Because suddenly, they return to cracking their throats, and the clamor of their common soul thunders again.

Ah... Of course –I think–, how are they going to silence the accumulated pain of all the women throughout history, simply with a song? They will have to keep expelling their guts through their mouths, for endless hours.

My eardrums hurt. My head throbs.

What else can I do to see their pain? I want them to shut up once and for all!

As I say this, in the sound space occupied by the women's screams, the child I was returns. That teenager who suffers and cries under the sheets is projected inside me again.
I address him, and in a soft voice, I say, "I see you, I hear you, I feel you, I understand you, I take you." I have nothing to explain to him. I don't want to convince him that everything will be okay. My teenager and my child, both, like the women expressing the pain of the roots with their screams, only need to be seen; they require my Presence. That genuine presence I didn't get from my father.

And I saw the pain of Man

One of the two women spells out loud once again: "Get-out-of-my-house. Now. Get out of my house!", as if blowing a clue from my story that I didn't catch the first time. On my right side, amid long spaces of silence, the Bear roars in pain again. It's tons of the accumulated and postponed suffering of Man.

I turn my head towards them. The "Get out of my house!" from one of the women still echoes beneath my skin. And... *Ah... Of Course!* It becomes evident to me that this claim I've been hearing is none other than that of my father, kicking me out of his house. It's a "core scene" from my adolescence that at sixteen, shaped the rest of my life. So (always aware, very consciously), I try to visualize my father to the right. I say to him: "Dad, how I regret when, with forced excuses, you convinced me to leave your house. That affected me forever." Then, I don't know where a question arises: "Dad, what is your pain?"

And he replies to me (I reply to myself), "Son, my pain is your pain; it's the same as yours. It's the pain of Man. It's the suffering of one who, unlike the Woman, keeps it quiet, endures it, postpones it, retains it."

This sentence, immense, now occupies all the space to my right: "Man retains the pain."

As I think about it, I become aware of my body. At this precise moment, I'm holding back my urge to urinate. I really need to pee, but I don't want to get up, interrupting this intense connection with my father.

Ah... Of Course! —I find myself repeating—. *After forty-something, Men have prostate problems. Life is telling us, "Everything you hold back, you'll have to let go... Now you'll have to pee all the time, throughout the night, release your pain."*

So, it manifests:

> ### Third Profound Understanding
>
> ***Man's pain is silent, and sometimes, it transforms into "absence."***
>
> Similar to Woman, Man experiences suffering, but unlike her, he endures it silently.
>
> Man holds onto the pain, refraining from expressing it aloud. It solidifies and persists. Occasionally, this "silent pain" can be mistaken for absence.
>
> In reality, many times it morphs into the absence of Man, causing him to withdraw from the family, children, and his wife. He becomes absent from life itself.

And now I see my father still floating to my right, looking at me, with a stealth tinted with absence... I return the gaze and say softly (to him and to the men who are screaming also to my right): "I see you, I hear you. I understand your pain."

Robert de Niro's grimace

In the midst of this hell of suffering, sometimes I find myself crying for the pain of others; other times, for my own. In reality, both are the same. Sometimes, I catch myself laughing at having gained some "Ah... Of Course!" insight about the human condition, or my own.

At this precise moment, I catch myself making that grimace of sadness immortalized by actor Robert De Niro, with the corners of the lips arched downwards, in a sort of "upside-down smile."

Tonight is not the first time I make this gesture; often, when I'm sad or frustrated, I notice that expression on my face, reminiscent of the actor's. And linked to this, another small yet significant revelation comes to mind.

Ah... Of course! This is also why De Niro is so famous. Because that gesture embodies the pain of the Man who holds back, who doesn't scream, who endures; the pain of the immigrant, an unjust victim of some war; the pain of one who couldn't save his family from famine or, if he did, had to leave his homeland forever.

That mark on the actor's face represents the impotence of failures, the postponement of the accumulated scream not only of his ancestors but of all men. Because we all suffer in the same way. All men identify with that brand of retained, "absent" pain. And, by extension, so do women through their sons, husbands, and fathers...

As I reflect on this, the spasms of the women persist, the Bear rests in its den.

The yellow cry

My body insists on reminding me that it needs to urinate. I don't want to get up from the mat; I don't want to remove the blindfold. But now I am fully aware that, by holding back the liquid in my bladder, I am retaining my pain, the pain of Man.

Thinking of my father, I also think of myself as a father. My daughter Alena comes to mind, and something that happened a week or two ago. At six years old, Alena has been wetting herself in class for several consecutive days. Nothing significant; obviously, we didn't scold her for it. When asked what was happening, her explanation was, "I don't like the school bathrooms" (she didn't like them those days; she always used them before).

This leads me to associate two premises of child psychology I once read or heard. One is that "when children wet themselves, they are almost always expressing something about their parents." The other is that "children heal through their parents"; that happens only when parents work on themselves and heal their own wounds and traumas. In fact, serious studies assert that many of the illnesses or pathologies of children are an expression of their parents' issues.

And what was once something insignificant now takes on the character of another small revelation at this moment of the ceremony: "Alena urinates to 'take' my pain." It's as if the little one is telling me, in that sometimes paternalistic tone she uses, "Dad, since you're holding it in and can't let it out, I'm going to take your pain and transform it into urine, out of love for you."

So, once again... *Ah, Of Course!* Alena wets herself out of love for me. She does it to show me something, to demonstrate that I must express my pain and not keep it to myself. She channels my pain; through some kind of process, an alchemy of love, she urinates it.

I know this sounds absurd. But that's what I'm feeling. And it's even more revealing to me, considering how I express love with my daughters. I do it, in part, according to what I received from my mother. Despite how violent she could be, most of the time, she showed extreme, clingy affection. My mother didn't want to "let me go"; she never wanted me to move away from "under her skirt." Alfredo, my therapist at sixteen, once told me, "Your mom wants to put you inside her vagina so that you never leave her side." And in a way, that horrible metaphor was true. On more than one occasion, my mother told me, "I want you to stay little, never grow up." She was always one of those overprotective mothers, overly intense in hugging and kissing, to the point of causing me repulsion. It's clear that mothers' expressions of affection cause rejection in their adolescent children. However, from my therapist's point of view, my mother's excessive affection touched on the lower limit of abuse.

With that "double-edged" experience, I am now very affectionate with my daughters. This is normal and pleasant; as long as they are little. And I can't help it; I love my daughters with all my heart. And sometimes it's as if love is bursting out of my chest, as any father would understand.

However, inside me, I recognize a bit of possessiveness. And the truth is that sometimes, like my mother, a selfish part of me wants them to stay little, not to grow up. Since they were little, I often tell them, "What is love?" And immediately I hug them tightly and add, "Love is this."

I do it as a way to teach them that love cannot be defined with words, perhaps only with hugs. But, once again, I sense that this is a bit exaggerated, an inertia of my mother's excessive affection. And if I think about it, it's even counterproductive. By teaching my daughters that love is hugs, kisses, and "don't grow up," "don't leave my side," probably, as a reaction, they will end up doing the opposite.

With the amalgamation of the image of the pain that Man retains, my bladder holding the urine, and the memory of Alena wetting herself, the master plant is revealing something much more intense than what is contained in the profusion of kisses.

Fourth Profound Understanding

Love is taking the pain of another, and transforming it.

Love is not (only or mainly) kisses and hugs. Maybe it's not even that. But now I understand that Love is (also), like my little Alena did for me, "taking" the pain of another and transmuting it. It is never about taking and retaining or keeping that suffering of others. No! It's about taking it and transforming it, eliminating it in some way. Alena's alchemy took the form of pee.

Now all this makes more sense. What do psychologists or therapists do, after all, if not "take" the pain of their patients and transform it into learning? What do Reiki teachers do but take the patient's negative energy, channel it, and discharge it? That is also a form of true love, even if there is a charge for it.

My body keeps asking me to urinate, and as much as I hate getting up and getting out of this trance of pure knowledge, I have no other option than to empty my bladder. Several participants are vomiting around me. Vomiting is, when taking ayahuasca, the most powerful symbol of "getting" the pain out of the body. But I don't feel like vomiting. I also don't have the impulse to scream (these women and men are doing it for me, in this kind of Family Constellation of my life).

Will urinating be my way of expelling vomit? Will I have to urinate on myself like Alena and thus take my own pain and transform it, transmute it out of my soul?

Making the decision to urinate in a room with twenty-nine people is difficult. However, convinced as I am that this is my form of expulsion, even lying on my mat, I make an effort to wet myself. But no matter how hard I try, I can't. I'm literally trying to pee on this mattress, but I can't.

I have spent several minutes trying without success; I have no other alternative but to get up and go to the bathroom, risking losing the beautiful feeling that ayahuasca is giving me now. I take off my mask and, with difficulty, sit up. One of the assistants notices my clumsy steps on the way to the bathroom and offers me his hand for support. I blink. I realize that having my eyes open is as beautiful as having them closed.

And I looked at the center

Back on my mat, I lose focus again. The sounds of vomiting and distress resonate in the darkness, and I have spent long hours flying with these spirits. But now the sounds are becoming more familiar. From the mouths of these two women to my left, a softer lament escapes, almost as it would have sounded in my wife's voice. I can almost recognize her unmistakable tone. Lying down, I turn my head towards her and observe, reflected in my black mask, Susana's suffering. "I see you, I hear you," I say to her. And in this position, I stay for another long moment.

I have observed and heard both the tumultuous grief of the women to my left and the silent anguish of the men to my right. It's enough. I am determined to continue my journey. And as a way to do it, lying down, I turn my head towards the ceiling.

My eyes are covered. The cries and retching, scattered throughout the room, surround me. Once again, I try to find the tunnel of my first ayahuasca experience to ascend and seek other answers, other levels of consciousness. But... nothing. The enveloping noise prevents me from following the path.

Looking straight ahead, I try to concentrate on the tunnel. Instead, an unexpected image comes to me: surfing; immensely high waves forming a tube before breaking in the middle of the sea.

I tried surfing only once in my life. It was a brief but revealing experience. I was on the Malibu pier with my friend Fermín; we were trying to learn to surf on our own. But after a few hours, we understood how naive we had been. We wouldn't be able to ride a wave on the first day without any instruction or experience. And just as I was about to leave the water, resigned to not even being able to stand on the board, a surf instructor appeared (perhaps wanting to promote his classes) and asked me, "Can I help you?" The instructor's confidence that I could do it filled me with joy. And although a bit skeptical, I accepted.

—When I tell you to paddle —he said—, you paddle fast; and when I shout 'stand up,' you stand up quickly on the board.

I did exactly what he instructed. And when I heard "stand up"... I surfed the blessed wave!

It lasted a few seconds. Due to laziness or the distance from my home to the beach, I never repeated it. But from that experience, I learned an indelible lesson: "Whenever you give up, what you seek is just around the corner" (or the wave).

This revelation also deserves the category of a Profound Understanding, even though it happened years before the ayahuasca experience. And now, amid the distraction of the screams, while I insist on finding my own path, my Inner Wise Self makes me relive that lesson. Also, at this moment, I realize that the T-shirt I'm wearing, bought specifically for the ceremony (we were asked to wear white clothes, and I had nothing of that color), is from Quick Silver, a famous surf brand. And I laugh to myself. I don't know why all of this appears to me as a peculiar response to the search for "my path," my center. Perhaps as a reminder that I shouldn't give up. I don't know. Maybe, as Freud said, "sometimes a cigar is just a cigar." Perhaps it's a clue that may still serve me tonight.

How much pain can I expel?

Why do they, both women and men, scream, and I don't —I tell myself— (yes, the screams continued in the air) *if I also feel pain inside me?* The answer is instantaneous: *They both scream for me.* I understand, once again, that this ceremony is a grand Family Constellation gifted to me by the universe.

I realize how presumptuous this sounds, but I am also aware that I am likely a similar actor in the constellation of the other participants. We are all connected. Not just the thirty of tonight, but all human beings. The traumas and pains are the same. We are branches of the same tree whose roots are our ancestors, the grandfathers and grandmothers of humanity, from the (supposed) first "Adam and Eve." This ceremony is a profound connection that began by mixing the saliva of others with mine, by all of us drinking the ayahuasca from that same little cup.

But the horrible howls persist, and no matter how much I look ahead, I can't find my path. Even believing that I have learned the lesson (by listening to the pain of the Women and the Men), I still can't see the tunnel to my next destination.

Will I have to scream too? Could it be that I'm not releasing my pain? Despite all the lessons, am I still holding onto it?, I wonder, and let out a long yawn. I open and close my mouth almost in slow motion.

My yawns, almost eternal, are a catharsis. Upon exhaling, I emit a sound of immense relief, as if I were purging my sorrow without sufficient determination or the need to turn it into a scream. Perhaps I am bidding farewell to part of my pain. And the shaman's words come back to my mind: "With each ayahuasca intake, you release a bit more suffering. But understand that you cannot take it all away. You can never completely eliminate sadness. A little bit of the pain must always remain. Otherwise, life would end."

Accepting these words, another great revelation of the day is born:

> **Fifth Profound Understanding**
>
> *Leaving a little bit of pain inside is necessary.*
>
> There has to be some pain within, to remember, not to repeat the mistakes of the past, of our ancestors. It's like keeping a history book always at hand.
>
> And when that small pain is amalgamated with the immense beauty of life, it becomes both present and insignificant. It's only there to remind us of where we come from and to guide us toward where we should go.

The smoke and the fear

During the introduction, the shaman warned us that, at some point during the night, the "helpers" would blow smoke from cigarettes with some type of natural tobacco. The idea, he said, is to create an effect of "discomfort" in us, to push us into the abyss of experience.

And so it is that, since I came back from the bathroom and covered my eyes to return to the depth of my journey, I feel a smoke that someone exhales on me, from my right side, the same one from which the Bear's roar came.

That smoke becomes too thick, and I realized that it is coming right from the side where, a few minutes ago, I was talking to my father; someone whose life had been shortened by smoking entire packs of cigarettes.

My reasoning, always on alert, tells me that the shamans must not be able to believe that I am so calm in the middle of such Hell. (Yes, the women keep screaming). *The helpers must want to make me vomit.* I imagine they think: *This one has to be taken out of his comfort zone so that he vomits, so let's blow a lot of smoke at him.* But even so, I don't vomit; I don't feel like doing it. My thing, I'm convinced, is to urinate on myself...

However, the smoke is affecting me, revealing something to me. Coming from my right side, from the place that my father's "absence" occupied moments ago, I remember that he was hospitalized with a pre-heart attack when I was barely nine years old. He survived, although not for long, thanks to a coronary intervention in which he underwent two bypasses. Nine years later he died from an aneurysm. From that moment on, smoke and smoking have taken on a threatening nature for me.

Relating these events makes me begin to breathe with difficulty, as if the oxygen in this room was consumed by smoke. No matter how much I breathe, deeply and consciously, I feel that the air is running out. And I make another association: the apnea that I suffer from when sleeping, perhaps has its origin in the smoke and the fear of ending up like my father.

In any case, and even though I understand it and know that I inhale and exhale without hindrance, now, lying on the mat, with my eyes covered, I feel like I can't breathe. So I sit up, take off my mask and say to myself urgently: *I must go out to the garden.*

I don't know if doing so is allowed or wise in my state, so I ask one of the assistants. The guy looks at the smoky surroundings. "Of course –he replies–. In fact, I would encourage you to get out." He accompanies me and with his hand, I arrive at the patio.

Behind, my father's absence still inhabits the gloom.

"Sit between my legs."

The night sky must have always been this beautiful, but I had never perceived it so fully. Not even during my frequent camping nights in the mountains. But in this house, nestled on a fresh hill, the air is so pure that even the stars can be breathed.

The contrast with the interior of the house is noticeable. So, I take a deep breath, gazing into the eyes of the stars.

I notice them like never before. They are clear, lively, amusing. *That's how they really are*, I reflect. The stars dance, literally; they move in all directions, leaving trails as if they were extraterrestrial ships dancing across the blackness of space.

But the most impressive thing is that I can perceive the connections between them! It's like seeing the patterns of the zodiac, the Ursa Major, and other drawings, similar to those shown to us in an observatory. And another little "*Ah... Of Course!*" comes like a shooting star: the one who discovered the traces of the zodiac in space might have done it during an ayahuasca ceremony or something similar. *How many masters must have written, painted, revealed truths to the world, sitting like me now, on Mother Earth, under the influence of the stars!*

I am outdoors and start to feel a bit cold. Next to me is a woman sitting on the ground, covered with a thick poncho. She reminds me of Mother Earth herself, Pachamama. It's Barbara, the kind lady who introduced herself upon arrival and chose the mat next to mine. I ask her if I can sit next to her to shield myself from the wind, and she points to a small cushion between her legs. They are open, as if she were about to give birth, with the small pillow ready to cushion the arrival of the baby.

Her invitation makes me feel very uncomfortable. *It's as if my mom were asking me to sit between her legs* —I think—, *to become her baby again, not to leave her side*. Or, worse yet, and the words of Alfredo, that therapist from my adolescence, resonate: "to get back into her vagina."

—No, thank you —I say without hesitation. And even though she insists, with tenderness, I can't help but feel a horrible rejection. Perhaps not to look bad, perhaps to submit to her charm, I'm about to do it, but I restrain myself.

—No, thank you. I don't want that now —I justify myself—. *I don't want to get between my mother's legs*, I think.

—But I'm not offering you anything sexual, just giving you a hug —she says with a surprised gesture.

I hesitate. How do I explain to this lady, without offending her, that this represents my obsessive mother wanting me not to leave her side?

—It's just that sitting there would be like being my mom's baby again. And I don't want that in my life. I'm sorry.

Barbara nods. I give her a loving hug, and she offers me a kind of blanket she has next to her. It's a Peruvian poncho, warm like a belly. I put it on without hesitation and sit on the floor. Dressed in the indigenous garment, I imagine myself as a humble shaman, sitting next to *Pacha*, observing the stars.

I'm in love with this poncho. And for some reason I haven't discovered yet, I feel it must have a lot of meaning on this night of darkness and fresh air. On the organic and impetuous earth, contained by this elemental garment, everything looks just as it is: perfect, harmonious, infinite.

I look up, where everything is even purer and more beautiful; I perceive the connections of the entire universe in my being; I see the stars and their evident dance, I can enjoy and dance with them.

The fresh air cleanses me of the smoke, but not of the truth.

After a while, a familiar force draws my gaze downward. Its weight makes me tilt my head. And from the depths, the fear invades me again. It's a sensation more horrible than the suffocation caused by the smoke in the room. And I sense that the approaching storm will be even worse.

Am I made for transcendent things?

Who knows how many hours and screams later, my mind focuses again on the moans that, only now I become aware, have never ceased. I hear how the moon cries, hidden, while the sun does not illuminate it. The birthing screams of women and the silent suffering of the father overshadow these stars.

Pain gradually takes over my present. But it's not just the pain of the soul; it's a fear that comes from the depth of the earth beneath me, as if it comes from a grave. Seeking escape, I look at the sky, but I can't reconnect with the stars. I think about entering the house. Then I remember that there is the stale air, my dad, death. *It's filled with smoke, and it will be even harder for me to breathe,* I tell myself. I have no way out anymore. I know that the only path I can take is downward. I must surrender to this.

But what exactly do I have to do? What does "surrender" mean in this case?

The lack of an answer plunges me into a kind of paranoia or panic. The mountain's fresh atmosphere, which I inhale with all my strength, no longer brings me oxygen. No matter how deeply I breathe, the air doesn't reach my blood. I worry about dying. But if I want to find the next tunnel, I must stay and delve into the fear.

So, I grab my feet with both hands. It becomes clear to me that this profound pain comes from my ancestors. *The roots*, I say to myself in a moment when pain gives me space to think, and something begins to make sense.

At the beginning of the ceremony, the shaman had warned us, "We can make a list of intentions for what we want to work on tonight. But know that these can manifest in unexpected ways. So it's good to keep them in mind, then let them go." And then he shared his: "Today, my intention is to work on my roots," he said while looking at me. And as I mentioned before, being Iván and I the only Argentinians (and the only Spanish speakers), I assumed that this would be aligned with his purpose. What I didn't know was that the theme of roots would play such a significant role in mine.

As I said at the beginning of this chapter, one of my intentions had to do with a "paradigm shift" in my life (the one of "Fight, fight, fight"). And that was the one I stated during the shaman's introduction.

However, at that moment, something else sailed the rivers of my mind, making me hesitate when speaking aloud. And although I decided that it was best to focus on changing that blessed paradigm, that something resonated in me: *Is it true that I am made for transcendent things?*

I have always had the vague idea that I am destined for "great" things. *Whatever I do* —I tell myself—, *I will have to help many people with it, have a beneficial impact on society...*

So, I at one point, I had the idea of studying at Harvard, or narrating Hollywood animated movies, or I even fantasized about making fortunes and being charitable to others... Until one day, my therapist Mauricio brought me down to Earth and told me that those "important" things ("Harvard", "Hollywood", "fortunes") were just "distractors" and represented more my mother's voice than one from the "beyond". "What you have to discover, –he said–, is what you really want to do; what your inner child wants to play."

When expressing personal purposes to the group, I would have felt ridiculous saying that I was going to ask the plant if I should "transcend," if I was some kind of "prominent man." And out of modesty, I exposed the "official" intention of fighting against my constant struggle paradigm. And even though my mind "slipped in" the other one ("Is it true that I am made for 'great' things? Or is it just my mother's voice?"), I left it there. I "forgot" it.

Now, the three intentions —the shaman's about roots, mine about changing my paradigm, and the one about my "delusion of grandeur"— come together in this terror attack under the stars.

In the uncontrollable pain that this underground presence causes me, Iván's purpose of working on his roots manifests in my own journey, like ascending hands that want to see the light. Then the shaman's intention merges with that "insignificant" one of whether I am made for great and important things. Like never before, I regret having planted that unconscious seed in the fertile soil of ayahuasca. And now, in the garden, embraced by my legs, a threatening voice resonates in me: "So, you wanted to do great, transcendent things?"

That voice no longer sounds as kind as my Inner Self's or the friendly shark from my first ceremony. It says with an otherworldly sound: "Then you'll have to let fear in and surrender to pain. But not just to your pain. YOU'LL HAVE TO DIVE INTO THE PAIN OF YOUR ANCESTORS. YOU'LL HAVE TO DESCEND TO THE DEEPEST OF YOUR ROOTS."

The fear transforms into terror! And the voice continues: "YOU WILL HAVE TO HEAL YOUR ROOTS, YOUR FAMILY'S, ALL YOUR ANCESTORS." This is too much.

"I can't. I don't want to. Enough!" –I fight, fight, fight, with my own Self–. I am very afraid. It's a very big responsibility, an extremely heavy burden!" I can't go on. I open my eyes, and I want to stop everything; get out of this state; I want to do what I know I shouldn't do in an ayahuasca session. And, of course, that makes things worse.

"I can't take the pain of all my ancestors –I shout under my poncho–. This is too much for me. Please, no!" But nothing changes. I remain trapped in this horrible purgatory where breathing is difficult.

Then, defeated, I try what I can no longer avoid. And it's what I believe "surrendering" to fear means in this situation. Broken, defeated, I say: "Well, okay. Show me... Where should I go? With my ancestors? To the deepest? Alright, I surrender, I can't take it anymore. If I have to die, so be it." I lean further, scratch the small stones on the ground, ready to dive into the depths of the earth. "There I go," I say. And let whatever has to happen, happen.

The place of fear

Another respite from the pain allows me to catch my breath. In front of me, a young man paces back and forth, impatient. He almost draws a groove in the earth with his feet. His steps are abrupt and theatrical. His cries are like those of a bear searching for food under the night's cloak.

I recall my night camping experiences. I usually go to the same mountain. Sometimes I go with my family, but other times I go alone. It's an area where there usually aren't many dangers, but the ranger always reminds me that there is a bear living nearby and that we shouldn't leave food inside the tent at night. And now come to mind those nights when, in the solitude of the tent, I would hear noises resembling those of a bear and would become frightened. Several times, in the middle of the night, I found myself with a knife clenched in my hand. Those sounds can be very real, sometimes even sounding like footsteps, very close, next to the fabric of my tent. But now, with no defense other than the poncho, "the Bear" is, indeed, in front of me.

And yet, I'm not scared. I know it's one of the participants; I even think I recognize Justin, wrapped in his blanket.

Ah... Of Course! –I understand, allowing the image of the beast to play in my thoughts–. This is the fear of the Bear that often invades me on those camping nights. It's not a real bear that prowls around my tent. It's a fear inside me, dancing out there, in front of my eyes. Fears never come from outside, from others; they are always within oneself. They only reflect in others.

The great paradox

What happened next has been erased from my mind; or perhaps nothing "transcendent" occurred. I only know that I entered the room. I suppose I got tired of suffering, or perhaps I unintentionally crossed the border of that fear from which I couldn't escape. I don't know. Maybe the panic and pain were so overwhelming that I thought: *Perhaps the smoke inside the house is not so bad, or isn't worse than suffocating in the fresh air.*

I vaguely remember that, before entering, I meditated on that other "intention"; the one to abandon the paradigm of constant struggle. I couldn't see the stars; I couldn't go deeper into my roots either, because the pain was too much. How could I bear to take on the pain of all my ancestors! I no longer wanted to do anything "big". It overwhelmed me. And I thought I should let myself be defeated in the battle.

Back on my mat, I try to put that sensation into words:

Fight, fight, fight. I wanted to change that paradigm and couldn't. I kept fighting until I gave up and accepted that I had lost the "battle" against "stop fighting." By accepting that I had lost, I stopped fighting; which was what I initially wanted to "change the paradigm."

I'm still trying to understand this paradox.

The truth is, like the Bear and the fears, the smoke was really more in my imagination than in the environment of this room. I confirm it now that, lying down, I hug the pillow I brought from home, and I feel like I'm floating like a baby, suspended in the universe. It's an inexplicable feeling of peace that embraces me in my dream. And I'm not asleep (I don't think I'll sleep all night).

I finally notice that the screams have ceased. Then I understand that when I was in the garden, trapped in that personal Hell, conditioned by being "made for great things," I came to convinced myself that "surrendering" to fear was plunging into the pain of my ancestors; surrendering to those roots that summoned me from below.

First, I had wanted to avoid it; run away. Then I believed that if I truly wanted to end that torment, I had to go down. I tried to deceive the plant, telling myself: *If I want to get out of this fear, I have to stop fighting and surrender*. But nothing happened.

I didn't realize that what I was confusing was one fight with another, and that the true meaning of "surrender" was not to take on the pain of all my ancestors and bury myself with them. It was to enter the house!, where the smoke was not real. Because the fear of suffocation was, like the Bear, only in my mind. "Surrendering" to the pain of my ancestors was a self-deception that postponed my paradigm, and I kept fighting and fighting. The three powerful intentions converged at that point on the black earth: "roots" and "transcendence" had intertwined with "fight, fight, fight."

Only when *I accepted to lose* was when I could enter the house and discovered that the fear of smoke had no reason to be; instead, a beautiful and deep sleep awaited me. Returning to the room was the real "surrender"! And by allowing myself to lose, I won that battle.

Fight, surrender, win, lose. The important thing was to stop wondering if I'm made for transcendent things or not. Fear, being internal, is as big as one believes it is; as much as our own pride magnifies it.

And I peed on myself

The urge to urinate and write pulls me out of this conscious dream. I don't want to get up. I'm so comfortable in this place! I have so much peace! It's hard for me to describe it without betraying this moment. So much understanding subjugates me while at the same time enlarging me. And I wonder, how can the wise tolerate that their knowledge doesn't make them more or better than those who "know" less?

In reality, no one "knows" more than anyone else. We all carry the entire wisdom within us. It just awakens. The mission of some might be, perhaps, to awaken it in others. And I say "perhaps" because the purpose of many may precisely be to experience simplicity, plainness; even misfortune. That's why the "wise," the "leader," or the "victor" aren't worth more or less, aren't better nor worse than their supposed antitheses. Moreover, it is likely that, for these, knowledge, victory, leadership are nothing more than tools of their avatar, or even cells of their own limitations.

I once heard something that sums it up perfectly: "Everyone is worth one (1) unit of Human Being."

So, I ask myself the question again in other words: *How can the wise tolerate that their knowledge doesn't make them better, not be at a higher level?*

Simply put, many are not aware of this universal equality. And therein lies their arrogance. This makes me understand that being "made for great things" doesn't hold more value, it is not better than being made for small things!

Pride is dangerous because one self-judges from it. And thus, you can fall into the error that greatness is better than smallness, that being a lion is better than being an ant. Or believe that being a farmer or a butler is less than being a Nobel Prize winner.

It's not just that none is better, obviously, and that all are necessary. What makes this even more evident is that most likely, it is ourselves, our Higher Self, who, from that Zone 3 (described in the first chapter), choose to be one or the other! We decide to incarnate in one or another avatar to play this game of life and experience what we lack. Perhaps the plumber has already been a spiritual leader. Perhaps the ant has already been a lion in another life.

Nevertheless, with my thoughts and the urge to urinate, I ask myself once again: Am I made for transcendent things? I don't know. I am made for things. I am made to play.

But one thing is certain. As long as I judge the ant as insignificant or compare myself to the lion, I prevent myself from living my identity as an elephant.

If in the first ayahuasca, I traveled to the Expanded Universe through a tunnel, tonight I can see that Expanded Universe from Earth... Where I should be. Accepting non-transcendence was what showed me the way out. I didn't have to overcome the smoke or immerse myself in the earth.

The only thing I had to transcend was... pride.

Happy with my incomplete answer, I sit up to continue my adventure. I go back out to the garden. I feel my feet on the ground; the poncho, now part of my skin. I look at the stars again, and now, with all the peace and a blanket of happiness over me, standing right here, I urinate in my pants, in the poncho, on the earth. *Pacha* absorbs all my pain.

And I dance once more with the stars.

To write or not to write

Happy, with my wet pants, I lie down on the uncomfortable little stones and begin to review each and every one of the Profound Understandings, the Revelations, the Words of Wisdom; all these words that have come down or that I have brought to my Being from some hidden place. The only fear that haunts me now... is the fear of forgetting them.

I embrace the enormous desire to write it all, but at the same time, there is a great abyss before me:

If I write, I miss out on living it –I reflect with concern–; *if I live it, I can't be writing it at the same time, and I could forget it.*

I decide to go in search of the notebook I brought with the purpose of taking my notes. I pick up a candle from some corner and settle back onto the uncomfortable ground. I can barely see what I'm writing. I just want to jot down brief phrases to later weave the story.

The real dichotomy within me, more than that of writing or living it fully, is:

Do I want to write (and publish)? Yes. But what's the point of writing all these "phrases of wisdom"? They won't help anyone! People have to feel, have to experience pain, have to see the pain of humanity; it doesn't help for someone like me to tell them. Also, while it's very nice to see all these connections between the stars and the like, I don't want to have to take ayahuasca to write the "truths." And if people have to live the pain, it doesn't make sense for me to summarize it in "universal truths"; which, after all, I'm not sure are so true or so universal.

While I write with the help of the reflection of an absent moon, I start to think about all the knowledge and wisdom I am absorbing tonight. It's so much that within me, I can't distinguish humility from pride.

Watch out! Believing that you are made for "grand and transcendent things" can expose you to that unbearable pain of all your ancestors –I remind myself–. *And, at the same time, feeling that what I have to say is worth nothing, or that I don't have the talent to convey it, can also be a deception.*

Then, another Profound Understanding emerges within me. It takes the form of a phrase that I still don't know if it's wisdom or plain absurdity, like in those dreams where you believe you're living a super-interesting movie and, upon waking up, when consciousness tries to put them into words, they no longer have greatness, creativity, or anything.

Even so, with some modesty (or courage), I put it down here:

Sixth Profound Understanding

Pride defeats itself.

It's a monster that bites its own tail.
I think I understand everything, and that makes me arrogant; therefore, I understand nothing. I must remove the crown, the last layer of understanding, to move to the next level.

And just as the night is closing in under the stars, so are the pages of my notebook. And I approach a promising dawn.

Yes, I'm going to *take* Mauricio

The light of dawn begins to enter timidly through the window overlooking the garden; the same garden that witnessed the passage of the Bear and my deepest fears last night. I realize that I have hardly slept. I am tired, and yet, I am not sleepy; I don't want to lose what is happening to me. That's why my mind is fixed on an internal debate: to take San Pedro or not.

In the days leading up to the ceremony, I have been considering whether, after the ayahuasca, I would dare to continue the journey with this hallucinogenic cactus. I had never heard of this type of plant or its effects. Especially now that the horrible night retreats before the new day, I do not feel the need, the urge, or the curiosity to drink it.

Nevertheless, perhaps I should try to surrender and trust once again in the shaman who has so lovingly guided us here.

I mentally review the ceremony program, which suggested:

Day 1: Ayahuasca (Mother or Grandmother) at night. San Pedro (Father) in the morning.
Day 2: The same, for a second time.

This means that the immensity of what I have experienced up to this point represents only twenty-five percent!

There is no need to reiterate the respect (and, honestly, a bit of prejudice) that I still have for drugs, despite everything.

I recall my first experience with the Amazonian plant. And I believe it is necessary to remind myself, in other words, of the conclusion I reached in the Sierra de Madrid. Given its relevance, I repeat it now, giving it the category of:

Seventh Profound Understanding

Drugs are not inherently good or bad; their qualification depends on the Purpose for which they are taken.

All human beings carry some form of pain within. We can blame others or numb this suffering with drugs or other addictions, or we can try to face it head-on, accept it, and work through it.

Most of us choose some form of addiction to "numb" or "anesthetize" this pain. Thus, depending on our patterns and personal traumas, this dependency can manifest as addiction to work, sex, video games, social media, alcohol, food, streaming series, and much more. Increasingly, people turn to recreational drugs. None of these elements or actions (work, sex, video games, food, social media, etc.) are inherently bad. Even medications are drugs, yet we use them for healing. Addiction to these and the avoidance of pain as a purpose are the problem.

One can use drugs to "numb" pain, to disconnect from reality, to flee from suffering and avoid confronting it... Or one can take a drug to connect. The former will lead us to continue "stumbling over the same stone," to keep, as it were, "repeating the grade" in which we find ourselves. The latter, on the other hand, will allow us to "move to new levels" in the video game of life, encountering new challenges; more problems and pain eventually, but at different levels.

Ayahuasca is a type of drug more conducive to being used for connection, precisely because by facing our greatest fears, it produces the opposite of an escape from pain.

However, even this master plant, when taken too frequently, would entail a certain escape from reality, from the game itself. Paradoxically, becoming too connected with the Source is to disconnect from our reality on Earth.

However, upon recalling this, I have serious doubts about whether it would be good for me to continue with the ritual and consume this second medicinal plant, which they call "Father" here.

I review in my memory what I have read in some serious publications. As I mentioned, San Pedrito is a cactus. Like ayahuasca, it contains natural substances with hallucinogenic properties. The potency of its effect depends on how "aged" it is in its process, and other details of its preparation. It was used by various pre-Columbian cultures, especially in the region of Peru. There is even archaeological evidence of its consumption for religious purposes dating back to around 1500 B.C.

And in the mix of plants and memories, the words of the shaman also resonate. According to his "personal recipe" (how he prepares it), San Pedrito "is much milder than ayahuasca, and its objective is to prolong the final effect of it throughout the following day."

Then, in some corner of my brain, as the power of ayahuasca recedes like a marine reflux, Mauricio, my current therapist, appears in my mind. I recall that session last Thursday when, with his Argentine accent, he said to me, "You don't take me, Gerardo, you have to take me." He was speaking of "taking" in the sense of apprehending, of absorbing what he was saying to me.

And this convinces me completely. I open my diary and write: "Yes, I am going to 'take' Mauricio. I am going to accept his 'Take me'." And the tide in my mind calms.

To convince is not to allow growth

It's early morning on the second day. I hold in my hands a large glass, filled with a light green powder. As instructed, I fill it with tap water from the kitchen. Stirring it is difficult; the cactus, in powder form, is thick and doesn't dissolve easily. With some effort, I gulp it down in one go, just as we were advised.

The bitter taste lingers on my taste buds for a few minutes, reminding me of the sadness of the previous night, whose meaning now begins to grow in my soul. All those human connections, which I've been perceiving like infinite threads linking the stars, I see even more clearly with an open heart. I'm excited to delve deeper into the universe of my Profound Understandings.

If the ayahuasca has been a present experience imbued with fear, this is a present time... and nothing more.

What would I do myself in the face of my everyday problems in this state of total connection and observation? –I reflect. Or in other words–: *How would I respond to those situations that cause me pain or distress if I saw them like this, without the prism of the mind that conditions (and sometimes even controls) my responses, my reactions to the external world?*

I then bring to this moment some of the conflicts that usually invade me.

I think of a very particular client of my company (let's call her Maria), who always demands more from us than agreed upon, not only presuming it to be free but also ignoring expressions like "please" or "thank you." I also think of a very willing collaborator of ours (let's call her Clara) who, precisely because of her goodwill towards others, tends to be susceptible to the abusive demands of that lady. Naturally, it's hard for me to tolerate that someone who doesn't respect the work and time of others (Maria) unfairly benefits from someone who puts her patience and willingness at the service of others (Clara), even beyond what is due, excessively. Faced with this, I often fall into a personal dilemma. On the one hand, I want to defend Clara, immersed in an unjust situation, but at the same time, I know that taking a paternalistic position with her is not healthy. And in my attempt to "not interfere" in her decisions about her own work, I usually suggest the arguments she should use against Maria. I do it, of course, as a way to "save her" difficulties, to make her task easier. In other words, I don't want Clara to "make mistakes" (not only because it would go against what was agreed with the client, but with a deeper meaning). And in that eagerness, I try to "convince" her to follow my strategy; to do what I would do in her place. The result is, now I see it clearly, that I don't let Clara grow!

This "paternalistic" attitude, this acting as if I always have the perfect solution, is a pattern I often repeat with friends and people who ask me for advice, or who share a specific situation with me. And that is so similar to what my mother used to do with me!; preventing me from growing, wanting me to stay "little" forever. It is very much alike, at the same time, to the attitude I sometimes have with my daughters, impatient for them to quickly resolve such and such conflict.

Am I helping Clara, my daughters, others with my intervention or am I getting in the way of their evolutionary path?

In this beautiful state in which my Being finds itself, I understand that I have to let them make mistakes, to follow their own path. Perhaps (and as I have found out several times) I will finally see that my suggestion was incorrect; that, just like my mom's, and despite the good intentions at play, my strategy was wrong.

Clara's situation is just one example that, as always, speaks more about me than about others. The more I detach myself from getting what I want, from "saving pain" for my daughters or anyone else, the more I allow others to make their own way and me mine.

Eighth Profound Understanding

Convincing, in some cases, does not allow growth.

Even disguised as defending or helping, many times what we do is try to impose our way of thinking on others.

And even though the result may be temporarily positive (saving them time or money, for example), we are preventing the other person from making mistakes. And since growth only happens by learning from mistakes, we are avoiding their growth.

This is part of my own Paradigm Shift. In the inertia of a life that involved "fighting, fighting, fighting," when I find a "solution," a path, a "reason," sometimes I want to implant it onto others to spare them the long journey I have traveled; to save them money, time, pain in the end.

But by doing that, I deprive them of a learning experience that might eventually even prove to me that my supposed "solution" was wrong. Both of us stop learning. And, in a vicious circle, in the effort to "spare them pain," I continue with my paradigm of "fighting, fighting, fighting," through reasoning and argumentation; to convince them not to waste their time...

The only way to genuinely "spare" pain for our peers and, especially, for our children, to clear their path, is by working on ourselves. In this way, far from "reducing" their pain to prevent them from growing, we avoid passing on our pain, our traumas... They will already have enough with their own.

I repeat: I must not try to convince others. Because convincing, in the sense of imposing my point of view, and even with the purpose of helping, does not allow them to grow.

Being Present for the Women in my Life

If the experience of ayahuasca during the night was a Family Constellation with the universe, from the depths of Hell to the stars, my heart tells me that this morning with San Pedrito can only improve it. Overflowing with enthusiasm in my mind as well, I am determined to make the most of this second day.

I begin by silently traversing this immense garden overlooking the mountain landscape, which grows even larger with each step. There is a girl reclining on a two-seater lounger. She is excessively thin. She must not be more than eighteen years old, and her name is Elie. Her gaze seems lost. But it is aimed at the edge of a stone. There a lizard basks in the sun, frozen in time like a statue. The little animal seems, from time to time, to return her gaze. And I feel a genuine impulse to sit beside her.

I saw her the afternoon before entering the room with her mother. I remember they are Russians. The impression they gave me when they arrived was that of the typical controlling and overprotective mother who, faced with her daughter's great sadness or trauma, brings her to "force" her to heal... (Something similar to what my mother did when she forced me to go to therapy when I was the same age as this girl).

Now, what I perceive in this lounger is a girl too attached to her mom and too distant from her dad. I think of a father perhaps "absent" (like mine), or even abusive. Who knows...

What emanates from her posture like a powerful aura is a profound "fear of Man".

Even though I perceive all this, I have the desire to sit beside her. For some reason, I want to help her; and I intuit that, by doing so, I can heal my own story.

But I still hesitate whether to approach or not; after all, she may not yet be of legal age. I am a man of forty-seven years old, and I wouldn't want my intentions to be misinterpreted. And so, after some back and forth, I sit beside her.

Her attitude speaks for itself; she is turning her back to me, as if afraid. "Don't come any closer to me, you've hurt us too much, both me and mom. You left; don't come back. I don't want you by my side." The girl hasn't spoken; I sense that she is "thinking" these words, while the lizard hides under the rock with a fleeting movement.

I shouldn't make her feel invaded. "I'm sorry I didn't ask if I could sit next to you," I say, to break the ice. She responds with an obvious lie: "No, I hadn't even noticed your presence."

After a long and uncomfortable silence, I ask her how her experience with ayahuasca has been. Elie tells me that, despite the screams of the women, she had a wonderful night. And with each word, she forgets the fear.

"I had a kind of conversation with my father," she whispers softly.

She then tells me that she hardly ever sees her dad (an absent father!), but thanks to the plant, she has managed to talk to him.

"We could laugh again. Both of us were laughing, happily...," she recalls, and this draws a smile on her face.

And as she says this, significantly, both of us laugh happily too.

In these slow minutes we share, only a few words were needed to achieve a familiar harmony... She needs a present father, but without abuse. And I need to realize that if I am possessive with my daughters, they could end up distancing themselves from me, just like this girl did from her father.

Elie, with her pain, only needs to feel that her dad is by her side, without invading her; just like I needed the presence of mine. And like me, she also doesn't need an excess of affection from her mother.

Immediately, I perceive in Elie some traits of my daughters, Emma or Alena; or both. And I hear, once again, that deep voice of my Higher Self reflecting: *Ah... Of course! They only need my Presence.*

Here we are, the two of us, the four, the six, all of us. As if I were Elie's present father; as if she were one of my daughters; as if she were me and I, my absent father, who is now present with his son, more present than ever. We are connected like this, in various ways, in various roles, in infinite planes.

I laugh with her and now I cry with her. I briefly tell her about my experience from the previous night. And I tell her that the pain of Man is silent and that, sometimes, it can be confused with absence.

For a moment, pride urges me to go deeper. I am intrigued to delve and discover if my hunch that her father has abused her is true. I review lessons, advice... I feel like I could hug her and tell her that I can be, on this sunny afternoon, her "present father"; the one she needs. And in the midst of everything I think to do to "solve her problem," I remind myself that: Convincing the other is not letting them grow.

Once again, I project her as one of my daughters. And I remember that love is not "kisses, hugs, not letting go, saving the other from pain, not wanting them to grow." I understand again that, as my daughter Alena showed me when she wet herself, "love is taking the other's pain and transforming it."

The lizard peeks its small head out again and makes one of its characteristic push-ups. At this moment, having listened to Elie, having laughed with her, I feel that nothing more needs to be said or done.

> **Ninth Profound Understanding**
>
> **They only need my Presence.**
>
> My daughters, Emma and Alena (perhaps all children), don't need an excess of kisses and hugs, an always insufficient and desperate love. They don't need my wish for them not to grow. They won't need me to do everything for them when they're teenagers, to save them time, money, and the pain of achieving it. They don't need that subtle and overprotective "abuse" my mother had with me.
>
> They simply need me to be by their side, to listen to whatever they want to tell me, to laugh with them, to advise them when needed, to let them fall, get up, make mistakes, or teach me that I'm wrong; to allow them to grow. "How difficult!" And yet, how easy:
>
> They only need my Presence. And nothing else.

With this phrase resonating within my being, with that deep understanding, I bid farewell to Elie. I sit under a sunbeam, on some rock, and open my notebook.

I write that perhaps, thanks to this Profound Understanding, I am healing future traumas of my daughters; avoiding that, by being a possessive father, they drift away from me and I end up being... an absent father.

How magical it is that one can, not only heal present traumas, but also future ones!

I hope I can live up to this, my Understanding.

Being Present for the Men in my Life

I'm about to resume my writing when I realize that I've lost the black ink marker that has accompanied me thus far. I search the house and find another one.

I sit under the sun, on any chair in the garden; I open my notebook and as I draw a line, I notice that the new marker writes in blue ink. Almost without thinking, beneath the first stroke, I note: "And now I'm going to write my life with a different color."

I lift my head and notice that, without intending to, I have sat next to one of the three young men I met yesterday. More precisely, next to David, the one who introduced himself with an intellectual demeanor. I hadn't noticed his presence until now.

Observing him and his posture, I notice he is on my right, sitting in a chair like mine, in an identical position to the one I have taken: left leg crossed over the right. And, just like me... he is writing in his diary.

He is not yet twenty years old. He is slender and handsome, much like I was at that age. His mirrored image makes me think that, in this Family Constellation in the universe, I am sitting next to my "intellectual teenager"; that young Gerardo who was attending university, who was popular among his friends and girls, and at the same time thoughtful and sensitive.

I have to find a way to engage in dialogue with him, murmurs my mind. The situation reminds me of that short story by Jorge L. Borges, "The Other" (which I had to narrate for an audiobook not long ago), in which an elderly Borges finds himself sitting on a park bench in Cambridge, next to the young Borges, and they both talk about their lives...

My reflection and I must be thinking the same thing; because he looks at me and offers a smile identical to mine. Then he shrugs.

This encourages me to speak to him; and I tell him about my questioning from last night:

—What's the point of writing, if people really need to experience pain? What good is it to narrate these Understandings or Truths, revealed during the ayahuasca, if people will only understand them when they suffer the pain and live a similar experience...? Also, if I spend time writing about everything I'm experiencing, I'm not fully living it; and if I immerse myself completely in the experience without worrying about writing it down, I fear not remembering it later to put it into words.

—And what did you do in the end? —David asks me with some concern.

I reflect for a few seconds and reply:
—Both things.

He smiles again.

From this completely non-judgmental attitude, born from my portrayal as a teenager, another response emerges within me:

> ### Tenth Profound Understanding
>
> ***I have to write, because people are already suffering!***
>
> We must tell the world that all that pain makes sense. We need to convey how necessary it is to experience the suffering of those who came before us; to see it, acknowledge it, honor it. To avoid turning "pain" into "suffering" and instead transmute it. And that even leaving a little pain inside is necessary.
>
> By the way, it is possible to write and experience. I'm not sure if at the same time, but both can be done.

I wonder if it's the fear of ridicule, or not being enough, or what exactly doesn't allow me to write or find a suitable format to do it. In any case, I don't think I have to take ayahuasca to receive these revelations. After all, it's clear that they don't come from outside but from within me. It would be very sad to have to depend on the plant for this.

Anyway, maybe this is a more personal Understanding than Universal.

But the experience will soon be enriched even further.

Another archetype of me

A few feet from David and me, Justin positioned himself some time ago; the same one who, in the midst of last night's Hell, was howling to my right; the same one who later walked restlessly in the garden, like a bear under the new moon. He must be the same age as David. An indigenous feather earring rests on his left shoulder.

Justin is practicing a mix of cathartic yoga and onomatopoeic dance. His dark complexion could well be the heritage of Native Americans or Mexicans, depending on which side of our border his ancestors come from.

I glance at David, who, like me, remains in the comfortable posture of the observing writer.

—He's exercising for us —I comment to David while raising my eyebrows and nodding towards Justin.

And my mirror returns another knowing smile.

But Justin is also an archetype of myself. He is that other teenage version of me from my twenties; energetic, emotional, and spiritual. *There must be something to uncover in him* —I imagine. But I still have much to discuss with this embodiment of Gerardo's intellectual and seducer persona.

I ask David to tell me about his ayahuasca experience.

—My main themes last night were my right shoulder, my penis, and a talent show in fourth grade —he begins—. Regarding the first, I've been suffering from pain in my right shoulder for a long time, and even though the injury I had has healed, the pain persists. On the other hand, I have a cyst on my penis, which I believe is because, some time ago, I decided to separate love from sex. I was dating girls just for sex, and I'm paying the price for that. And finally, at nine years old, in school, I didn't dare to participate in a talent contest because I thought I didn't have any talent. Those three things came up during my journey with the master plant.

For my part, I not only see in David a "teenage version" of myself, but in some way, I project myself as his father. And by extension, I become the father of that young intellectual and womanizer Gerardo: in other words, my dad.

Perhaps that's why I feel compelled to say to him:

—I sense that your themes may be connected to the masculine and paternal part. In Biodecoding, and in other studies about the 'messages' given to us by different parts of the body, the shoulder is related to the burdens and responsibilities we take on. The right side of the body is associated with the father. And the penis, the quintessential male symbol, as well.

—You know, that's exactly what's present in my life these days —the boy says, dismayed—. Healing the relationship with my father and, above all, helping him heal. My dad has suffered a lot, and thanks to everything he endured, I have an easier life.

David also confesses to me that his father did an ayahuasca ceremony with him for the first time just a few weeks ago. This last story moves me, as it intensifies the "coincidences" of the moment.

—That's so cool about your dad! I wish I could have done an ayahuasca ceremony with mine... —I say, with moist eyes.

It's enough to say it to realize that... I'm doing it right now! I'm experiencing this ceremony with my dad!

In this wonder of cosmic connections, which are now flowing openly to my awareness, David is my teenage self; and I am my father. Of course, I'm having an ayahuasca ceremony with my dad! But I'm also my internal father, the father of my teenager, doing an ayahuasca ceremony with my own inner teenager, reflected in this mirror. I am the father of myself, and I am present as never before for this teenager, David; and also for that Gerardo who, at sixteen, had been kicked out of his house by his dad...

David looks up, thoughtful, and with a smile of joy, he reflects:

—Yeah, my dad is so cool.

Embodied in him, the teenager inside me is also saying how cool *I* am.

There are so many layers of existence in this conversation that are like facing mirrors casting multiple reflections; all of father and son; dad and me, David and his father; me, the father of my inner teenager...

This young man beside me is the redemption of that sixteen-year-old Gerardo, wounded by his father's absence. And I am the dad that David needs; a dad who listens to him, happy, present.

"They only need my presence," I whisper, so that only the boy inside me can hear me. David nods with a smile of deep understanding. And we both resume the posture of crossed legs and writing in our notebooks.

I wonder if he's been thinking the same thing as me. And in doing so, Justin's panting interrupts my meditation. The dew still refreshes the morning, and in all this time, the other version of my youth continues his energetic yoga, his restless bear-like movements. He is also a crystal that reflects another image of what I was; a Gerardo at once hyper-kinetic and spiritual. Both David and Justin are my doubles from adolescence. I was smart and handsome like David; muscular and mischievous like Justin. Clear as the dawn, these two images teach me something about my life and perhaps heal something of theirs.

Now Justin is massaging and tapping himself on the lower back. It's the same ritual I've been doing for years (and even more frequently these days) to ease my moderate but continuous lower back pain. I look at him and remember one of the questions I put in my intentions ("What does my back pain mean?"). Years ago, a computed tomography had revealed two dislocations in my fourth and fifth vertebrae. Looking closely at Justin's back, I notice he has two spots, two moles, at the exact height of those vertebrae. The similarities with my story extend to these details that, to my rational mind, sound ridiculous, but in the midst of the magic of this ceremony, I have no doubt, they hide an exact science.

And it's David now who repeats, as if the time I've been observing Justin hasn't passed:
—My father is so cool.

I point to Justin, tireless in his primitive dance, and reply:
—That cool?

Without turning his head, David furrows his brow. He looks at our friend and answers:
—No. Not *that* cool —and once again, we merge in our complicity.

I want to go further, discover more about David and his reflection:
—Perhaps you, like me, are intellectualizing your father's pain.
—How? —he replies.
—Look —I say—, I've spent almost my whole life with a kind of paradigm: 'Fight, fight, fight.' It's about approaching an everyday situation as I were at war, constantly arguing, using reason, knowledge to

convince others, as if I were at all times a "defense attorney" for myself. And I do so, in part, because my father was often "absent" from my life and left me at the mercy of my mother's madness, without certain defenses, exposed.

—Uh! —my young double exhales. And he adds—: That is exactly what I do.

A brief silence follows his words, lingering in the air.

Healing through each other

Suddenly, Justin ceases his fire dance and stands still. It's as if he has stopped feeling the music beneath his feet. He slowly lowers his head to the ground and begins to water it with childlike tears. He mutters something, inaudible despite the short distance between us. With his back to us, he cries almost silently.

I feel the urge to approach. I do. I take barefoot steps that allow me to stand by his side. *What can I say to him without intruding?*, I think again. I don't know if he needs a hug as much as I do... I put my hand on his shoulder.

That's all I do. I feel the perfect muscle of his arm and the sensation of placing my hand on my own shoulder, that of that energetic Gerardo from my twenties; the one who, in his fragile vigor, holds the fire of anger and pain.

Justin sheds tears, interrupted only by short sobs. His face is red with anger.

—Are you okay? —I manage to say.

When he can regain his speech, he murmurs with a thread of voice:

—Last night someone approached my mat and covered me with a blanket. That made me feel at home.

Now it's my eyes that moisten.
—You're home —I feel like telling him, and I do.

Then Justin reveals the impossible to me: His father kicked him out of his house when he was seventeen!

Although he doesn't use exactly those words, what he tells me has an identical meaning. He continues:

—My dad treated me like a dog. He slept in the bed and threw a blanket on the floor for me to sleep like an animal.

Empathy for him descends into my throat. And I confess to him:

—My father kicked me out of his house at the same age as you; and that has marked my life with fire; it was one of my main themes in this ceremony.

With deep compassion, I add:

—I am healing through you. I hope I can serve you for your own healing.

I hug him. I express a wish that is almost a certainty within me:

—You will find your own dad within you, and you will give a home to that boy. You will make it.

I want to tell him many more things. Things like please be careful with that "homelessness" he feels, and with that feeling from last night, of "being at home" in the midst of this ceremony, as he could easily be confused and fall into a cult or something similar.

Once again, I am overcome by the urge to spare pain for the other person; to smooth their path. I want to warn him, I want to protect him; I seek —as I do with my wife Susana and with so many others— to spare him the mistake, to avoid the frustrations. Unintentionally, I am trying to hinder his own learning process.

And when, in time, I realize all this, I fall silent. I give him another hug and I withdraw, carrying with me, frozen, those moments of my two adolescences:

> ***Eleventh Profound Understanding***
>
> **They only need my Presence.**
>
> As the father of my inner teenager, I am giving Justin what his father has denied him: the conscious presence of a dad who is there to help you, to protect you, to give you a home. In talking to him and David, I am really talking to that teenager within me. Just like with Eli and my daughters, there's no need to intervene in their growth processes with rigid advice or overprotection. I was with them, sitting by their side. That's all they need. And also, all that I need, my wounded child, the teenager within me, or our children... They only need your Presence.

The psychoanalyzed psychologist

Every single person participating in this journey is a part of me. Just approaching one of them is enough to feel those threads of energy that bind us, like the stars of last night. Each one represents some part of my personality or my Being; precisely the parts that my mind needs to heal. The connection is clear and direct, incredibly powerful.

I wonder if I should keep digging and searching for more connections.

What I've obtained has been so intense that it already overwhelms me! Should I continue connecting with the other people in this ceremony? If I decide to stay for the second day, would it be driven by the pride of knowing more? If I choose, instead, to go home, would it be out of fear of encountering another torment of pain like last night?

At times, I look for the shaman. Ivan and I have only exchanged a few words yesterday and a few more this morning. But what I want is time with him to tell him all of this; I want his support, his guidance. And yet, every time I look for him, he's listening and helping someone else.

Right now, he's talking to a participant with whom I've exchanged very few words. I know he's a psychoanalyst and Belarusian, living in Ukraine. He arrived from that country yesterday, hours before the ceremony. I don't remember his name. His physical resemblance to my psychologist, Mauricio, is incredible: thin, a couple of days' beard, short hair, and thick glasses.

Right now, he's sitting in front of the shaman, both immersed in a deep conversation. The image, as I perceive it, is that of a psychoanalyst being psychoanalyzed. He's telling the shaman, in a highly reflective and deliberate tone, something about his life or his experience last night.

It piques my curiosity, and I approach. I sit next to them. In a regular situation, this would have been an intrusion, but in this context where we all feel part of the same Being, with our hearts open, it feels perfectly appropriate.

From his "divan", the psychologist is recounting something that seems more like a reflection than a question:

"I always have my ex-girlfriend in mind; a relationship that was very important to me. She was calm and spoke slowly; she had an inner peace that I couldn't quite understand. At that time, I was working in my practice with psychedelic drugs, and I also consumed them. My girlfriend didn't, but she still supported me. I remember once we were on a train. I have the image, repetitive and constant, of the incessant 'chug chug' of the locomotive. She was sitting in front of me; with that peace, unreachable for me. Suddenly, she blew me some kisses. And that made me very angry; it was something I felt for no reason at all. I don't know why, but it made me mad. I had that internal anger, which she didn't have, and maybe that's why our relationship didn't work out."

The shaman responds that perhaps her peace was "apparent." That may be she also harbored her share of anger, albeit contained. Or it was possible that that girl simply couldn't satisfy his anger.

I step away from the conversation and write: "Susana can't satisfy my anger. The rage I feel is against my mom!".

I must admit that, in addition to the physical resemblance to my psychologist, and the similarity of his story regarding the relationship with my wife, in this case, I am not able to see beyond. At least, not like I did in the interactions with the Russian girl or with my teenagers doubles. However, I know that, within me, that clear connection with my own anger will continue to simmer slowly until the answer is ready.

Meanwhile, in the kitchen, Mrs. Barbara pours herself a tea.

"Kid, you eat for all the hunger in Africa, hey!"

Something struck me as funny. The psychologist (who, in this Family Constellation in the universe perhaps represents my analytical part) is, as I said, thin. The teenagers (Justin and David) are too. The Russian girl is to the extreme of anorexia. Even the shaman has a slim figure.

Among the people I've had contact with, only a couple were obese. One, a financier I spoke briefly with. The other, that very friendly, big guy, John ("Little John").

I exchanged a few words with "Little John" during the introductions. He talked to me about how much he likes Argentine meat, how poorly he was handling the fasting before the ceremony, and how much he wanted to eat a "tira de asado" (barbecue rib). I have no doubt that he represents my compulsive overeater part.

It's lunchtime, and those relationships between thin and fat are feeding my mind.

After more than a day of fasting, and several on an "almost" vegetarian diet, the floor of the room is covered with the most exotic and delicious dishes one can imagine; all lovingly prepared by Nicole, the official chef of the ceremonies.

I find myself on a threshold that separates ravenous hunger from satiety. I feel like I could devour all the dishes on the menu, or eat nothing at all. I don't know which of these impulses I'll encounter, how my mind will react to lunch. I don't expect to have healed my addiction to eating by any means, and I understand that my stomach is closed by the natural effect of fasting. Nevertheless, I experience that fear that, if I taste the food, I won't be able to stop.

In my eagerness to control the experience and make the most of it, an idea occurs to me: *I'll take a plate and offer "Little John" to share it. What could be more healing than sharing a plate with my other 'self', the compulsive overeater?*

But the master plant has its own plan, and it's not our minds but our Inner Wise Sage who controls the situation.

Just having that idea is enough for Barbara (the lady who last night played the role of my mother, sitting outside with her Pachamama poncho) to reach out to me with a small plate. In it, there's barely half a sweet potato and a few grams of a delicious salad sprinkled with seeds. It's none other than the representative of my mother (who is obese and a compulsive overeater, perhaps even more than me) in this group who is offering me the food.

In the slow passage of the tiny plate from Barb's hands to mine, I reflect on how healthy this symbol is for my own addiction. I see the image of mom telling me: "Here's the food that nourishes you, so you can nourish yourself, but don't overeat." This is what my heart wants to hear.

After the slow movement of her hands, I take the plate, observe it for long minutes, sitting on the floor, without tasting its contents. I feel a deep respect for this food. An aura of humble reverence washes over me, teetering on the edge of tears. From my eyes, they cascade freely, soundless and unbound. In this delicate moment, they descend, suspended between hunger's ache and the whisper of fulfillment.

Finally, I savor the dish. With the fork, I invite the immensely small pieces to float into my mouth, in slow motion. I don't want to do anything else. With my head bowed to the ground, it's almost nothing that I put between my lips. It's a departure from my usual manner of eating. This is nourishing. I don't need more food to do it. And amidst tears of happiness, of love, but at the same time of compassionate sadness, what I sense is... the hunger of the world.

I don't feel it in my stomach, but in my heart. I am deeply grateful. I feel humble, embraced by the clods of the earth; my bowed head is a reverence to it. And I bow with joy, gratefully acknowledging the poor, humanity, my ancestors who went hungry.

Randomly (or not), a couple of memories warm my soul. One of them is a passage I read in a book by Ken Follett, "Winter of the World," which takes place in post-war Russia. The author recounts that in the years following the Second World War, the famine was such that in a country where potatoes grow like grass, the Russians were fortunate if they managed to swallow their peel. And not only that, they made entire meals and recipes just with the skin of the tuber! As I carefully appreciate the skin of this sweet potato on my plate, I remember having cried, years ago, when reading those events narrated by Follett. Now, the story feels deeper and closer to me.

The second thing that comes to my mind is a voice, that of my Aunt Mary. During my adolescence, when the kind woman saw me devouring like a caveman, she would say, "Nene, vos comés por todo el hambre de África, che"[1] ("Oh, kid, you eat for all the hunger in

Africa, hey"). "Stop a bit, you're going to choke." Her everyday and "rough" wisdom was, at the same time, infinite; as great as the modesty that now floods me when, with my head bowed, while everyone enjoys the unexpected feast, I savor the food slowly, feeling how it satisfies and nourishes my whole body and being.

How strange it is to be experiencing all of this! –I tell myself–, *to feel these truths of the universe without arrogance. It's hard not to feel it when one delves into their personal development and discovers such knowledge. Because the more I understand, the more arrogance pushes me. The more you know, the harder it is to taste humility. How do you swallow this great paradox? How?*
"Like this" (I laugh inside). And I continue eating, in tiny little pieces.

How impressive it is to enter humility through food! The word "humble" comes from the Latin "humus", which means "earth". Food comes from the earth. And I, with my head still in a position of gratitude, pupils fixed on my tear-soaked feet, understand it more than ever. I leave the plate almost full, aside, and a voice interrupts my reverie.

—Could you pass me my water bottle, please?

As I turn my eyes, I discover a pair of black feet. They belong to a young man in his twenties, Ron, whom I haven't seen since yesterday. I trace his skin (completely dark, like the night) up to his head. A *rasta* hairstyle rests on his shoulders. The whites of his kind

---

[1] The words are intentionally accented, following my Aunt Mary's Argentine accent, since that is how they sound in my experience.

eyes contrast with the rest of his slim, muscular body, beautiful in its healthy blackness. I follow the direction of his gaze; to my right rests his water bottle, next to mine. Immediately I recall that yesterday, noticing that his bottle, made of metal and with a black lid, was identical to mine, I pondered: *Uh... With the Covid virus on the rise, I hope not to confuse myself in the middle of the ayahuasca and drink from this guy's bottle.* And a few minutes later I was drinking the ayahuasca from the same glass that twenty-nine people had used before me!

I hand him his bottle and confess my concern about accidentally swapping our saliva. And he responds with a shrug: "Everything ends up in the same place."

Then the advice of my adorable Aunt Mary echoes again, as if she were speaking to me from beyond: "Kid, you eat for all the hunger in Africa!"

This guy, of African ancestry –the third version of my inner adolescent who presents himself this afternoon–, clearly represents that continent, and the hunger of my ancestors, and those Russians from the post-war period, and all those "for whom I ate" gluttonously in my adolescence. Those for whom I compulsively eat in my everyday life, perhaps foreseeing an imminent scarcity. I did it and I do it perhaps, in part, because of the ancestral memory of dozens of Spanish, Italian great-great-grandparents, who suffered the helplessness of not being able to feed their children.

By associating my Aunt Mary's phrase with my interaction with this young African-American man, who is now sitting right next to me, I have the urge to comment on the "coincidence". But what's the point?

I decide to continue my journey and lose sight of him.

Now, in the kitchen of the house, I join a small line to refill my water bottle. While waiting my turn, Ron – the same young man I was talking to moments ago– appears behind me and asks: "Is this yours?"

He's pointing at a plate with leftover food on the kitchen counter. Indeed, I recognize that it's the one I was eating from minutes ago. It's still almost full. Someone must have put it there to be washed. "Yes, it's my plate," I tell Ron, "but I'm done eating." With the utmost naturalness, he takes it. He doesn't care that it's dirty, used by someone else. He adds a little food for himself and returns to his seat.

His simplicity and humility make me reflect. Where I see a "dirty" plate, he sees a plate with food. I don't think Ron is poor. He has more awareness than I do.

When I return to him, this time I can't help but comment. The water bottles, the plate of food... those are too many "coincidences" already. I know I'm not going to end my addiction like this, as if by magic. But I want to share with him, to find out if there's more to learn.

With some embarrassment, I mention my Aunt Mary's phrase that resonated in me a while ago without noticing his presence. I tell him that he, in a way, in my story, represented the hunger of Africa; that our bottles were the same; that then I had ended up eating from my "dirty" plate. In the end I say to him: "Last night and all this morning I was finding deep connections of my history in each of the members of this group. I honestly don't know how relevant or insignificant this 'coincidence' with you is... But I had to mention it."

Ron smiles kindly, without adding anything. I ask him how he processes the ayahuasca experience, and he tells me that he does it "singing, with music, with rhythm"; that that is very important in his life. I still don't know if there's more learning for me in his words, although I sense it. For now, I know that I want to eat like this every day, enjoying every bite, honoring the hunger of the world.

Another healing to the future

While I'm talking with the African-American version of "my teenage", right behind me is my mat. The only reason I'm not sitting on it is because it's been invaded by two girls.

One is Elie, the Russian girl I talked to hours ago in the beach chair. The other is a girl in her thirties, pretty, slender. Her name is Viktoria. She's also Russian, but unlike Elie, she looks like those women who need to appear strong, perhaps to defend themselves from men.

Elie and Viktoria aren't sisters, but it's evident that (besides their origin) some invisible bond unites them. Both are on my bed, and that immediately projects the image of my daughters, Emma and Alena, in about ten or twenty years.

The older one, Viktoria, holds the head of the younger one between her legs, who looks pale, as if about to faint. Sitting on a nearby mat, the mother of the younger girl, also Russian, participates in the conversation.

Elie is of slender and fragile build. While Viktoria strokes her hair, I hear them talking about anorexia or bulimia; something the older one seems to have suffered and advises her "protégée" about. The topic makes me pay attention. Although on the opposite end, my problem of compulsive overeating is also related to food. I feel like I have to contribute something from my experience to this conversation, something that will be healing or helpful for these girls, and also for me.

I move a bit closer, infiltrating their circle. Viktoria keeps talking as if I weren't there. But I notice that, in the unfocused space of her gaze, she registers my presence very well. And even though I sense some resentment in her attitude, I try to speak. Before saying a word, as if she had read my mind, Viktoria abruptly silences me: "I'm telling *my* story," she says, with that kind of false hatred with which children disguise their tenderness. "OK," I stutter. "I'm sorry." And I continue listening.

I notice that Viktoria is eating one of those delicious baked potatoes from the menu, and as she does, she sets aside the peel. I recall the passage from Ken Follett's book, the post-war Russia. Both are Russian. Another "coincidence"!

I interrupt them again by saying to Viktoria, "If you're not going to eat that potato skin, can I have it?" Once again, as sharp as before, she says to me, "No, this is *my* food." And she takes the peel into her mouth.

"I think what I want to share with you can contribute to your story," I insist, determined to enter the conversation. "I'd like to tell you. If you'll let me." She then lets me into her circle.

I disclose to them that I'm a "compulsive overeater," and that our pathologies are related. I share with them my memory of Ken Follett's passage and the post-war Russians ("Possibly your grandparents or great-grandparents," I relate to them), of how they used to prepare entire dishes with just the potato peel. Perhaps there's something of the famine of their ancestors interfering in their present.

Viktoria, Elie, and her mother now listen to me attentively. The first, who seems to have lost her aversion towards me, says that her father constantly spoke about the post-war hunger, and that he always ate what was left on his daughters' plates, so as not to waste anything. Moreover, he was always scolding them to finish their portion. And she adds, "One day, I saw a photo of my dad when he was young and said 'Wow, he was thin and handsome. And now he's so fat!'"

"What you're sharing is exactly what I do with my daughters," I confess to them, and amazed, I tell them how I try to force Emma and Alena to consume all their lunch or dinner, and end up eating what they leave on their plates "so as not to waste anything." "In fact, last week, before getting home, I forced them to eat, in the car, all the lunch I had prepared for them for school; I didn't let them get out until they did," I add, while remembering (now with sadness and shame) that scene of fury.

"No, don't do that ever again," Viktoria warns me, alarmed. Then she falls silent for a moment and I think she's going to start crying, but she shakes her head and continues.

> *"That's how my father caused me an eating disorder; and I suffered for many years. Let your daughters serve themselves on their plates the amount they want. Nobody knows better than oneself how much they need to eat; not mom, not dad; nobody!"*

The emphasis she puts on this last sentence allows me to understand her initial impulse to evade my presence. But even more deeply, I understand the message of this moment.

It's not just about my healing from my compulsive eating problem. No. It's something that feels somewhat foreign to me, yet it's equally, if not more, important than my own journey.

Then it's revealed to me:

> **Twelfth Deep Insight**
>
> **You can heal the future!**
>
> In this conversation with Viktoria and Ellie, both with anorexia, I am learning, I am healing a future problem that I have been creating for my own daughters, with my actions!
>
> When one puts time and energy into working through their own traumas, not only do they heal themselves, they are saving time and energy for their children. They are preventing them from having to work through and suffer from traumas that are not theirs to bear. They will have enough of their own. Why delay them on their path of growth?
>
> Now I see even further. I understand and accept that, perhaps, there may be problems that I'll never heal; not with a thousand ayahuascas or ten more years of therapy. Maybe the deepest sense of healing is to heal those who come after us, our children and grandchildren; to gradually reduce pain, generation after generation.

Therefore, from today onwards, whenever the opportunity allows, I will ask my daughters to serve themselves what they need to eat. Of course, I cannot let them choose their type of food (or they would only eat sweets and mac 'n cheese), but they can choose *how much* to consume.

I will no longer force them to finish their plates. I will no longer eat the leftovers.

Viktoria's recent words are a message from the future; as if they were spoken by my eight-year-old daughter when she reaches her age. As if Emma, this afternoon, from a future moment, were teaching me how to feed her.

Aren't the connections we humans have wonderful? If only we could see them clearer, more often, without needing ayahuasca... how much more beautiful the world would be!

Meanwhile, the other girl, Elie, now with the color back in her face, tells me why she had taken my place. Oh coincidence! The spot where my mat is now is the same one she occupied in her first ayahuasca ceremony, two weeks ago.

In my profound understanding, I become her father again, the one now occupying her same place (mat). Elie and Viktoria, just like my daughters Emma and Alena, seek refuge in daddy's bed; a father who, in Elie's case, is as absent as mine was; a father who, a few hours earlier, on the two-seater lounge chair, had shown her that he was present; something I needed from my father.

I stop here because I don't want to seem crazy. But someday, or in some other dimension, surely we will be able to see these "coincidences", this magic, through some scientific device; some "computed tomography" that scans the recesses of the soul.

Pravda! (Truth!), I write in my diary after finishing my conversation with them.

The bodybuilding musician

I wander through the house and find an open door. Inside, a muscular man in his fifties is playing the guitar. Like with most participants, we introduced ourselves yesterday. However, I don't remember his name; I do remember he's Brazilian and I was surprised by his well-developed muscles, cultivated to perfection. Every fiber of his body is worked in a spectacular, almost cinematic way. In fact, as I mentioned before, he resembles the character "The Incredible Hulk" in the latest Hollywood version. He's big, with green eyes, handsome, and his skin is evenly bronzed. Although I wouldn't want to look like him, it makes me think of the opposite of my image, with my extra weight and lack of exercise. And I must admit, I feel a bit envious.

Upon entering the room, where I believe the bodybuilding musician is as much of an intruder as I am, I find myself, as I do with everyone in the group, addressing him as if I've known him my whole life:

—I didn't know you played the guitar.

Well, how could I know, if I barely know him! He, engrossed in the instrument he's barely strumming, asks me if I play any.

—Uh... I'm taking piano lessons, although I really don't know much about music. I think, for me, music is a transition to a new stage of life, where I want to discover my artistic sensitivity —I reply.

He continues, without paying attention to anything other than his guitar. He scratches the strings a bit more. From his gestures, some Rolling Stones song must be playing in his mind, but the instrument sings something different.

—I want to hear something more cheerful. What's playing is too depressing —he says.

The "depressing" thing is the meditation and peace melodies emanating from the speakers in the house.

—Well, don't expect them to play a Rolling Stones song in this place. But you can play something happier.

—I love Frank Sinatra —he confesses, furrowing his brow; and I remember the lyrics of "My Way," the only song I ever heard my mother sing.

—Do you know how to play 'My Way' or another Sinatra song?

—No, they're too depressing —he insists, and that makes me think even more about my mother.

Through some mysterious connection, there are two things filling the air in this room: my mother (with Sinatra and her lifelong depression) and the music. Is music my path to stop eating compulsively, to the "perfect physique" like this Hulk's? Is music, for me, vanity? Or health? These are just questions hanging in the air, of which I don't have the answers. Ron, the black guy, had also told me that he processes his ayahuasca experience by singing...

But there's a third connection with the bodybuilding musician (whose name I still don't recall); something that will be revealed at the end of this journey...

Once again, the Pride

I continue searching for the shaman around the house. He's always attending to someone else, and I can't find him available to talk. But at this moment, I cross paths with him, and I'm surprised to see him pass by with a concerned expression. I follow him, and he stops in a secluded area of the house where some of the attendees and the shamaness who lives here are gathered. Everyone seems agitated. I notice that one of them is hiding something in the attic. When I manage to reach Ivan, I ask him if they need help. He responds that police helicopters are flying over the house, and yes, I hear the whirring of the blades. I look out the window. They are literally meters away from the roof, as if searching for something important. It's understandable that the homeowner and the others are nervous.

I offer my help again, and someone asks me if I can lend a hand in removing "things" from the house. My impulsive response is that they can count on me, although I don't think moving "merchandise" is a good idea. I'm still in a state of pure love, but my mind is taking control and starting to focus on the situation. I deduce that a neighbor has reported to the police the tremendous screams that flooded the night. Luckily, the other participants are still enjoying their respective experiences in infinite peace and tranquility, without noting the overflight of the metal bird.

Someone from the organizers' group reasons that perhaps the police don't know exactly which property the screams came from. Maybe they're just trying to "stir up the hornet's nest." I, without any authority, dare to give an opinion: "I would advise not to remove or hide anything from the house; let's just act like nothing is happening." And I add, "The helicopters up there are *searching for* something. We down here are also *searching for* something." I don't want to sound wise or arrogant; just helpful. But I sense that now is not the time for wisdom, so I step aside.

The police surveillance increases my doubt about whether to stay another night or not. Although we're not doing anything wrong, I feel a slight paranoia creeping in. If the police come with a search warrant, what would be the most appropriate action? Could the notebook I'm writing in be considered evidence? Obviously, I wouldn't destroy it; it's too valuable to me. I fan the pages looking for something that connects it to its owner.

On the first page, it says: "Gerardo Prat - 1st Grade." I smile; it's something I wrote a long time ago, joking with one of my daughters. "Look, just like you, Dad also has a 'First Grade' notebook," I told them that day, pretending to be a child. I hadn't realized I had brought the same one as a ceremony diary. And with the innocent idea that "the evidence" cannot incriminate me, I tear out that page. As I tear it, I think: *Am I actually graduating from First Grade today; from some First Grade of life?* I dispose of the paper scraps in the trash. Now nothing identifies this notebook with me; except, in reality, everything.

Fortunately, after a few minutes, the helicopters abandon their search. We, however, continue ours. I look for Ivan, who has disappeared again. *Why is it that every time I want to talk to him, he's not there for me?,* I wonder with more mystery than frustration. Each of the participants reflects a piece of my history, an aspect of my personality, and I'm very intrigued to discover what part the shaman would represent. Ivan isn't like those gurus who talk to two or three people, just to simulate closeness, but then "enlighten" with their absence. He's one among us. He helps everyone. He listens more than he speaks. He doesn't abuse his wisdom.

I write: "The shaman is the equidistant point between humility and pride. It exposes my own pride. I won't be able to go further until I balance these two extremes within me." As I feel this warm humility in my heart, that arrogance spins around the crown of my head. Maybe I don't deserve more understanding. I don't know if I should stay one more night. If I do, I'll continue discovering the other members, finding connections with them, and knowledge will keep feeding my pride. But if I leave without completing the second day, would I do it out of humility or out of fear that tonight the plant will force me to face another test, an even tougher one, an idea that terrifies me? And if the screams repeat, will the police come, and will I end up in jail?

Since dawn, I've been pondering this dilemma. The day is coming to an end, overflowing with answers. But there's none for this pressing question.

Whose poncho is it?

While meditating, in the oasis hanging from this mountain, I saw a blue-crested bird gliding over the cliff, ignoring the wind. Elongated walnut leaves approach me at intervals, propelled by the western breeze, which doesn't whisper the answer I am looking for.

I could have asked for the opinion or advice of each one of those here. But what good would it do? Whether I should stay or leave for one more night is a decision that lies within me, nowhere else.

If I could, I would pose the question to my therapist, Mauricio. In a session where I asked him, "How do I know what's healthiest for me in every situation?" He replied that when I wasn't sure what to do, I should question myself: "What would Mauricio tell me?", because usually, his responses to my conflicts are what my "healthy and wise Self" would do.

I even thought: *What if I ask the Belarusian psychologist (who physically resembles Mauricio)?* The fleeting thought left with a smile. Then, kindly, I summoned my Inner Wise Sage and said to myself: *What would Mauricio tell me?*

And like rubbing Aladdin's lamp, as I pronounced those words in the silence of my mind, the Whatsapp bell on my mobile phone rang. In the ephemeral notification —the one that only appears for a few moments on the screen— I managed to see that a message from a certain "Mauricio" had arrived. But what intrigued me the most was that it came from the chat of this ceremony! *How is it possible that my therapist is sending a message within this group?* —I ponder, feeling perplexed—. *It's impossible! Could it be a product of the ayahuasca, a mere hallucination?* I begin to fear that possibility.

The notification has already disappeared from the screen, so I check my communications with Mauricio. There are no recent messages. I then check the ceremony chat, and indeed, there is a message sent by someone named "Mauricio"! It simply contains a photo of the landscape I have in front of me at this very moment: the hills, the sky of the beautiful sunset in Topanga Canyon.

Before I go crazy, I remember Occam's Razor Principle, an ancient technique used by detectives to solve complex crimes, which says: "Other things being equal, the simplest explanation is usually the right one."

So there must be a Mauricio, whom I don't know, among the twenty-nine people in the ceremony. And if the photo was taken from this same garden, that Mauricio guy must have been very close a minute ago when I asked myself the "magic question."

Without further deductions, I ask someone: "Is there a Mauricio in this group?" And that person replies to me: "Yes, the Brazilian guy." *Ah... Of Course*, I say to myself. And I go after the bodybuilder musician.

As I said before, we introduced ourselves yesterday, but in the wave of new people, I hadn't registered his name. I scan my surroundings looking for the bulky amateur musician (by the way, Mauricio, my Mauricio, besides being a therapist, is a professional musician for a lifetime). I know that no one but me has the answer to whether I should stay one more night or not. But who can resist the opportunity to ask the genius of that accidentally rubbed lamp? If not as a decree, at least I'll take his opinion as a clue.

A few meters away, the bronzed Hulk admires the panoramic view, his green eyes lost in the distance. I approach him and cannot help but tell him what just happened. He listens to me mention the amusing "coincidence" and smiles thoughtfully. And when I say "therapist," he points out something curious:

—Therapist —he says, and then breaks the word in two— The-rapist.

Mauricio, the bodybuilder, hints that the therapist is a rapist! Trying to find meaning in the clever wordplay, I remark:

— You know, you're right. In a way, therapists "violate" our privacy, but to help us heal...

And I move on to what I really want to ask him:

— What do you think, should I stay one more night or should I go?

— I'm not staying —he tells me. I'll leave at sunset. I've had enough. I feel satisfied.

And he doesn't give me an answer; just like a good therapist would have done.

Something even more curious strikes me. Of the thirty people here, Mauricio is the only one leaving. Everyone else will stay one more night. *Still* —I tell myself—, *I won't let myself be influenced, not even by*

Mauricio; the choice is within me. And I continue to debate my options.

Although I still have a couple of hours left, I must make a decision soon. If I take too long the time for the second ayahuasca ceremony will arrive, and it will be hard to leave this place.

During one of my tours of the house, I come across Dina, the shamaness who lives here, and briefly talk to her. She explains that, if I wish, I can take a small dose; "maybe half a glass." And this turns out to be the middle ground I was looking for to convince myself. I then decide to stay to experience one more night.

Back in the garden, now freed from the extensive debate, I sit and breathe in the fresh evening air. I look for the walnut leaves. They are gone; the wind has changed direction. Before the moonless night envelops us again, someone interrupts me. It's time to hand over our phones again.

Like yesterday, we must leave them in a bag until tomorrow. I've heard amusing anecdotes, and at the same time disastrous ones, of what someone can do with a mobile phone in the middle of an ayahuasca ceremony; from that participant who wrote to an ex-boyfriend to tell him how clearly she now saw their relationship, to the other who started filming the exposed souls of the other participants.

Since I don't plan on doing any of those crazy things, I deposit my cell phone in the bag. I just want to put on "my" poncho and prepare to be protected from the next Bear. A smile caresses my soul as I recall the beautiful relationship I formed last night with that indigenous blanket, which warmed me and made me feel part of the earth. I was so attached to it that I was tempted to steal it. I said, "I could buy another poncho, but it won't be the same. I want this one." Then I gave myself another option: "I won't steal it; but I can take it with me and then tell the homeowner that I did it by mistake, and that I'll donate another five new ponchos, just like it (which won't be this one, so special)." Even to everyone I crossed paths with last night and throughout the morning, I asked if the garment belonged to someone in particular or if it was "just another blanket" in the house, like the ones offered to all participants. No one knew if it had an owner.

Only this morning, the heat of the sun forced me to detach from it. And since then, I don't know where it is. But now, faced with the threat of the night and its fears, finding it has become almost an obsession. I'm scouring every corner of the house; I've rummaged through all the ownerless blankets and even opened some closets. And finally, I find it. It's on a mat that I overlooked. I take it, borrow it once again, as if it were mine. I put it on. And happily, I prepare for a second night of ayahuasca.

In the kitchen, I run into Barb, that maternal-looking woman who handed me the plate at noon today, the one who last night, sitting on the ground, offered me the poncho. I'm trying to lovingly apologize to her for refusing to sit on the small cushion she had between her legs last night. I also try to tell her about my experience this morning with Elie. I tell her that my mother has been too affectionate with me, and that I tend to be equally affectionate and tender with my daughters. But in the context of my experience, what I feel I must do with my daughters now is to be present in a different way; that "they only need my presence," and that love is not just kisses and hugs... Barb doesn't understand me. It's as if I'm rejecting her own idea of love; as if I'm fighting with my mother's wishes.

Suddenly, someone taps me on the shoulder. I turn my head and meet the bronzed complexion of Mauricio, the Brazilian bodybuilder-musician, namesake of my therapist.

—Excuse me, Gerardo —he says in a soft voice—. I'm leaving now.

—...?

Amazed and without thinking of anything else, I start to open my arms to embrace him, as a sign of farewell. He agrees to my gesture, but he stays there, as if waiting for some other response. Until he finally tells me:

—It's just that I have to leave, and well... the poncho is mine.

Embarrassment makes me feel naked. I take off the poncho and apologize.

—All this time, I thought it was just another blanket in the house —I apologize. And as I hand it over, I refrain from mentioning that I've shed tears, wiped my nose countless times, and even urinated on that piece of cloth.

—It's okay. I brought it to share. But it's my daughter's, and I have to give it back because, as I told you... —Yes, Mauricio had decided to leave.

At that precise moment, as the group prepares to form the circle to begin the ceremony, I say to myself: *Enough. No more going around in circles. Mauricio is leaving, that's the answer.* As I say it, a powerful sense of satisfaction washes over me... and a genuine desire to leave.

In reality, what I feel is the true message of my Being. It took a lot to listen to it. It was hours of debate, and the answer was all this time within me; it's just that I covered it with the noise of the mind.

One night of ayahuasca hasn't made me feel "complete." No. I suppose being "complete" would mean having released all the pain, and that's like being dead. Now I realize that I, like Mauricio, am "satisfied." There's no correct solution to the doubt of staying or leaving, just as there isn't really one to any question. Everything, even the most "wrong" action, even the most "bad" consequence, is an opportunity to see something better. And the decision we consider the most "correct" can take us away from the necessary and inevitable change, from the game of living.

Everyone is already sitting with the shaman. The second night of the ceremony is about to begin. Without saying goodbye, without interrupting, I turn around and leave through the kitchen, making my exit quietly.

As I get into the car, another surprise forces me to go back. I've handed in my phone! I turn off the engine and retrace my steps, though not my decision. I re-enter the house almost on tiptoe. I search the closets and corners for the bag with the phones. Nothing. Filled with shame this time, I have no choice but to interrupt Iván's introduction to retrieve my phone.

There won't be a second night for me. I'll return home to my wife and daughters. As I walk back to my car, Mauricio puts his daughter's poncho in the trunk of his car.

The Bear and the Squirrel

What covers me now, as I drive back home, is a cloak of nostalgia. It's for those people in whom I discovered a bit more of myself, and whom I have just left behind. It's also for those with whom I didn't speak, and who surely would have revealed other pieces of the puzzle to me. I barely said goodbye to some. They were all representatives of my Family Constellation in the universe, and I couldn't thank them enough.

Although twelve hours have passed since I drank the second plant, the San Pedrito, and I feel capable of driving, my Being still floats, lightly, outside of my body. I have emotions close to the surface, and a relaxed mind. It's hard for me to return to material reality, to drive on the 101 freeway back to my house. That's why I stick to one of the slower lanes. *Maybe that's how everyday life should be* —I reflect—, and I can imagine it. Amidst the fleeting traffic, I almost feel unprotected. Fortunately, a huge truck gets in front of me. I stay behind it, moving slowly, letting it guide me like a father for the rest of the way.

I thought I'd find Susana, Emma, and Alena at home. But it's not late and the three are still at a friend's place. When I open the door, I feel something threatening in the emptiness of the house. And fear grips me.

It's a fear of the "empty house", which now feels familiar to me. It's the same sensation I had when I lived with my mother and sister in that small apartment during my adolescence; when mom would leave for her evening high school classes and leave me alone. That sensation, I can feel it palpably. Those nights, I'd cook for myself and, alone, I'd eat and eat endlessly in front of the television; unable to fill the empty apartment. If I go further back in time, the feeling is the same as the fear of a ghost hidden in the darkness.

Now the urge to eat returns. The loneliness, the hollow house give rise to that vicious circle of my adolescence. I eat something, but just a little. I don't want to ruin the sweet experience of today's lunch in Topanga Canyon. I still don't dare to turn off the light and go to bed. I prefer to wait for Susana and the girls to arrive and I sit down to pass the time.

I'm taking some notes when suddenly a noise startles me. It's much smaller than the one from the Bear. It sounds like a dog or a possum eating something in the backyard. It could even be a smaller animal. Perhaps it's the sound of a squirrel or a rat nibbling on a branch, amplified by the silence of the night and the plant still running through my veins.

In any case, it's not a common noise in my house; neither is its exaggerated volume. Sometimes I perceive a rodent sharpening its little teeth on a beam in the attic, but this is much louder. And it's coming right from the other side of the hallway door, the one that leads to the side yard.

I approach, and the noise grows louder. Whatever is causing it, is inches away from me. I don't even want to entertain the possibility that it's my imagination; that would scare me even more. But I'm perfectly aware and the noise is real. *Perhaps I'm too aware and perceptive*, I tell myself. I think about opening the door but, I confess with some embarrassment, I can't bring myself to do it. A few moments after accepting this, the noise disappears.

I think of the supposed Bear I hear outside the tent when I'm camping. Could it have also been the fear of loneliness in that completely empty apartment during adolescence? Perhaps my own internal childhood fear has magnified the small noises in the echo of this darkness.

The next day, as usual, I pass through that side yard, and I hear a noise. It comes from a plant just behind the door I didn't dare to open yesterday. As I move its branches aside, I see a squirrel staring at me and immediately, it scurries away, frightened, up onto the roof of the house.

In the afternoon, two friends, Mara and Fermín, come to visit us, expecting me to recount my experience. Susana and I, along with them, sit at the table in the other patio, in front of the house. As I narrate, summarized, this entire story to them, and just as I'm speaking about the shaman, suddenly a thunderous crash explodes on our table.

The first thing I imagine is that someone passing by the sidewalk has thrown a stone or some other projectile at us. But immediately, Fermín, perplexed, informs us that it was a squirrel, which fell from the tree above us. The weight of the little animal, increased by the force of gravity, landed right on the table, to fall on my friend's knee. The four of us are paralyzed. What are the odds of a skillful squirrel falling from a tree?

A few weeks later, when I narrate this anecdote and all the previous ones to my therapist Mauricio, he tells me something very valuable: that vomit represents anger and pee, sadness. He interprets it as part of my "paradigm shift". "You're transitioning —he says—, from adolescent anger to the sadness of the child, and that's very good."

Now I realize that, beneath the fear, whether it's the external magnitude of a bear or a squirrel, lies sadness. But the fear hasn't entirely gone away. Perhaps it's that little piece that, like pain, must remain inside one so that it can be remembered, to avoid repeating the same mistakes as the parents.

A small fear that hardly feels, amidst the beauty of life!

An "unfinished conclusion"

Upon finishing writing these pages, about an experience that lasted almost two whole days, I wonder: *What is the true healing that it has brought me?*

If I focus on the short term, I recognize that I haven't stopped eating compulsively, that some of my fears, anger, and sadness still persist. If I delve a bit deeper, I notice that, indeed, even in this brief term, some of all those afflictions have disappeared. Even if it's just a little, the symptoms of my profound pain have been alleviated.

I want to believe (and I do) that, in the medium or perhaps long term, the learning will provoke in my Being a permanent change, a healing. Furthermore, I know it. Deep inside, but I know it.

Still, the harsh critic living within me tells me something like: *Didn't all this knowledge cure you once and for all? Shouldn't you already be a wise man and a Master?*

It's a voice difficult to silence, like those screams from Hell. But neither it nor they are bad, they are just pain. And it's good that a little pain remains, as we said before, to remember, to avoid repeating. Mine is more than a little. There's a long way to go; it's a video game with many levels.

Perhaps humility is —and it's hard for me to write what follows— recognizing that I may never heal many things that torment me today. Maybe, for example, I may never stop being addicted to food. Maybe I can't avoid what I fear so much: that being unable to control this addiction will be the cause of a death foretold.

If so, was this experience just a distraction, another escape?

I reckon not. Because I believe that one's mission is not only to heal oneself and "level up." While that might be an important aspect of life, there's an even more important one: healing the future.

Perhaps I won't manage to eat moderately and become that wise, centenarian old man I imagine. But I'm convinced that, for example, through conversations with Viktoria and Elie, I helped heal future traumas of my daughters, to make their path easier. And this is something quite different from "saving" others from pain (as mentioned in that Eighth Profound Understanding), not letting them make their own mistakes. It's, as I also said, about sparing our children from bearing the consequences of *our* pain; reducing their suffering so they deal with their own, a little less contaminated with ours.

I think of those scenes from Medieval movies where they are calm in the village and suddenly, a man must rise from the table, take his sword or a simple axe, and go out to defend everyone from an invader. He does it as an obligation, accepting the reality that, whether he likes it or not, if he doesn't take up his weapon, the enemy will rape his daughters, will kill his whole family. Thus, with acceptance or resigned to this being, perhaps, the last time he sees them, he gets up, bids his loved ones farewell as usual, and goes out to face the threat.

It's a scene we've seen in dozens of movies, but I see it differently. I think: *That man is my great-great-grandfather! Or myself, if we believe in reincarnation.* I can imagine the terror it would give me to have to do that now. Stop writing this and wield the sword, perhaps never to return. It terrifies me but, above all, it saddens me. Because it's real. Some ancestor of mine, some grandfather or grandmother of the reader, did exactly that.

They accepted their burden, like somebody today defending... the rights of whales. They did it so that we, today, can embark on other battles, like gender equality or environmental protection.

That's what the entire spiritual evolution is about. Our ancestors lived deep pains, wars, hunger, sorrows we can't even imagine. They cleared the path so that we can focus on fighting the fears of our century; or simply work on our personal, therapeutic, spiritual development.

In conclusion: we cannot avoid affecting our children with our pain, stop creating traumas for them. Maybe we won't manage to heal ourselves. But we must try, to heal those who follow us. And do it even if we don't have offspring. Do it for the new generations of that tree, of which we are all branches or roots. So that each of them, in the future, may be happier.

THE INTEGRATION

Unlike my first encounter with ayahuasca, the teachings of this second experience didn't crystallize as much in the days and months following, as they did during the experience itself. What in the first experience had remained more symbolic (the shark, which was the gateway to fear) and which I later understood better over time ("Fear will not harm me"), in this second experience happened immediately (like "Profound Understandings") during the ceremony. This was partly thanks to the effect of the San Pedrito, which maintained the magical connection among those present in the ceremony, thus extending that final taste of the ayahuasca. And this is what I learned in the following days:

- The integration of the master plant goes far beyond what one learns or experiences in the ceremony. For example, I saw that Bear (Justin) walking in front of me, and I discovered that "fear is always within." (When, recently, I returned to the same campsite where I heard the bear behind the tent screen, it occurred to me to ask the ranger if the bear had appeared recently. To which the camp host replied, "It hasn't been seen for weeks. It's believed to have been hit by a car on the highway." So, not only did I stop hearing those noises from my Bear, projected by my fears, but literally, the bear that used to inhabit the campsite is no longer there! It's a change that occurred on several levels: in the ceremony, in the forest of my mind, and in reality. Isn't that incredible?)
- The connection between other people and our stories is astonishing. I had already experienced it in Family Constellations sessions, but this time, it was perceiving the threads that connect us in the matrix of the Fourth Dimension. Each person, regardless of their culture, language, appearance (neither the Russian girls nor the African guy seem to have anything to do with me), has an invisible bond that connects them to another. That connects us. Our stories, our families, our cultures, are all related. And even though there may be hundreds of thousands of years between that ancestor who left Africa and me, who was born in Argentina; even though I may have only one percent of that person in my DNA, we are

connected. Simply because, in the universe, millions of years are a second.
- Wisdom and arrogance are a snake biting its own tail. The more I understand or "know," the more I need to detach myself from my wisdom. If I let myself be trapped by the belief that I am wiser than others, I will only become more foolish and ignorant.
- Many believe that they have nothing to heal, that for them, it's not necessary to "pass to the next level, level up." Some people try to live without doing anything to self-discover, to improve as individuals. They believe they are exempt from having to dig into personal shit, authorized to live their lives on autopilot. Or maybe they think that because they had "normal" parents, their pain is incidental. The message of this ceremony for me was very clear: If one does not want to progress for themselves, they must do it for their children. And if they don't have children or nieces/nephews, for the children of humanity of which they are a part. Because what we do not heal, our descendants pay for with pain; a pain that, although important for them to learn, we have the obligation to alleviate.

PART III

*Reaching the true choice
Desiring and Wanting*

THIRD INTAKE OF AYAHUASCA

JUNE 11 AND 12, 2022

Between what I desire and what I want, lies the key to the Self. While **what we would like** *may be influenced by our traumas,* **what we truly want**, *as adults, as the gods we are, can only be uncovered from the pure center: our Inner Being. It is there where what I want and choose resides, beyond whatever my desire may be; where I feel that "I am my home." And from that place, all that remains is to decide, happily assuming the consequences of our choice, whatever it may be. In the third and last ceremony, that dilemma came to me as the fear of homosexuality.*

The Basement

Today, Friday, is the last day of school for my daughters, who are graduating from their respective grades. Alena is finishing her first grade; Emma is completing the third. And as I pick them up from school I think: *What grade will I pass to today, in the school of life?* Because I'm about to embark on my third ayahuasca ceremony.

This time the date is in the city of Pasadena. I arrive early. And as soon as I enter the house, I begin, both literally and metaphorically, to open doors.

The residence is of colonial style. All the walls, ceilings, and doors are painted in pristine white. Inside, there is a spacious living room whose floor will, in a few minutes, be scattered with mats, blankets, and buckets for vomiting. Three arches divide the possible paths to take: the left one leads to the dining room; the right one, to another small anteroom. Both converge in the kitchen. A central arch gives way to the stairs leading to the upper floor; and above it, an old wall clock.

In my curious journey, I try to map out in my head the exits and entrances, the bathroom, the garden. I know from experience that at night, the house could become a maze.

I notice that inside the bathroom (accessed by opening one of the white doors) there is only a small candle. I think that, in a few hours, its light will not be enough, so I bring another one from the kitchen to ensure I can see in the dimness. I mark the bathroom on my mental map and continue.

Before going up to the first floor, I try one last door. The daylight only allows me to distinguish three or four descending steps. Further down, my gaze plunges into a dense darkness, descending into the "subconscious" of the house.

Immediately I become aware that this could play a trick on me at night. *Oh no!* —I murmur to myself— *what if the fear represented in this basement appears?* I know that when fear comes in the ayahuasca dream, there is no other way but to surrender to it. *What if surrendering means going down to that black underground?*, I say to myself.

I hope not to have to open that door, not to encounter it tonight; or at least to forget its existence. Fortunately, that will be the case. This basement will not appear in my experience... However, I will have to go down to an even deeper and forgotten one: to my own basement.

The third day of the rest of my life

Just like in previous experiences, my therapeutic work with Mauricio throughout the year is fundamental. That previous process was, in a way, what shaped the intentions I set before me in this third ceremony. Mainly, these were three:

To bring order into my life. And to do it in various aspects. Perhaps the most important is to avoid oversleeping, which often results in not to being with my daughters in the morning to make them breakfast, or having free time afterward for my creative spaces. In that "sleeping" –by the way– is where I encounter my mother's depression, who slept until very late in the afternoon all her life.

To learn to act more from my "adult" self. To be a "parent" to my inner child. While in most situations of my life I act as an adult, in others (more than I would like) I end up doing something that is not good for me because some trauma intervenes between what I would prefer to do and what I actually end up doing. Oversleeping or overeating are clear examples. But there are worse ones. Sometimes it seems like fear chooses for me; I tend more to react than to respond like an adult. That is, I end up acting from the wounded child or adolescent. I am then invaded by that anguish we all know, which has no real reason. Especially on occasions that require big ethical decisions, I can end up betraying my values out of fear of "being left unprotected." Or, worse, out of "seeking a home outside of myself" (the home from which my father kicked me out at sixteen).

To achieve a fuller relationship with Susana, my wife. Although we have a happy life together, each one is, lately, immersed in their own creative project; she in her music career, and I trying to write. That often leads us to be out of sync. And especially her; looking more at herself than at the couple.

These three "intentions" were the key and the guiding axis of my entire experience, although they would appear arbitrarily, without a linear order, during the first night. The sensations, colors, and revelations would manifest themselves on multiple temporal-spatial planes, lost suddenly to be reintegrated in the following phase. And to explain them, words are merely primitive instruments.

Nevertheless, tracing a faint chronological line allows me to reveal in a more or less coherent way those visions, teachings, and even the most intimate thing that can happen to a human being: to see in front of oneself their deepest fears.

According to my conservative formula (which had worked so well for me in the previous ceremonies), as soon as I set those three intentions, I tried to let them go, to receive "what the master plant has to teach me today, as far as it is healthy for me."

I was about to do just that when Susana appeared.

Having knowledge of the healing effects of ayahuasca through me (although still afraid to experience it herself), she said that at the same time of night when I would be starting my journey, she would be meditating. "Since this is also going to affect me, maybe I'll receive a little healing incidentally, *as a rebound effect*," she said, half-jokingly.

Perhaps that's why I had included that "intention"; to achieve a greater connection between us.

Now, about to open the door of my heart to ayahuasca, and in the midst of introductions, the girl who was sitting on the mat right in front of me introduced herself and said her name: Susan.

Like all of us and like the walls of the house, she was dressed in white. I wondered what other "coincidences" would unite me with this woman, who had the same name as the person I've been sharing my life with for sixteen years. Later, I would discover them.

Definitely, Susana's intention must be the most important of the three, I assumed, believing I understood everything, forgetting, once again, that the conscious mind controls nothing in these ceremonies. There are no shortcuts to our purposes in them. In fact, just as "Hell is full of good intentions," failure is packed with shortcuts that fork toward it. Drugs to disconnect are shortcuts. Medicines to escape pain are shortcuts. Even ayahuasca can become a shortcut to death if we want to know everything at once, if we want to connect all the time instead of living in this plane that we choose.

There are few situations in life where shortcuts are necessary, preferable, or simply an option. Generally, it's about following the long, difficult path. Not in the Judeo-Christian sense of living necessarily the pain of guilt, but following it to grow slowly. If you want to hurry too much, life will let you know.

The same goes for ayahuasca. As I mentioned more than once, although one may want to heal something in particular, our Inner Wisdom knows better than anyone what we need to face at the moment. Even what we need to learn *before* addressing that point we want to work on. In this case, the message from "The Grandmother" was: "To improve your relationship with Susana, you will have to work on other things first..." And it took me on the long road.

To dis-order to order

Reclined on my mattress, with covered eyes, my aura begins to feel bigger and bigger... or heavier; primitive words, as I said, do not suffice. In this room, only the old wall clock continues to count the time. Someone starts burning sage, and the scent of incense fills every corner. I uncover my eyes for a second, looking for any windows to open, but then I realize it's just my paranoia with the smoke, and I return to my position. The room is silent. Contrasting it in my mind with the Hell of the second experience, this silence alone gives me peace. A soft, emotion-inspiring music rises, and upon it, another symphony begins; the symphony of vomiting, spaced around me, starts to uproot the initial fears.

I don't feel the urge to vomit. Perhaps I'll try, as in previous experiences, although I wonder if the fact that I never vomit is due to my strong stomach or because I always find another way to purge the pain. In the first experience, it was the immense yawns; in the next one, urination... Will I vomit, finally, tonight? Or is it that my pain is so stuck to my guts that it cannot be released?

I try to think of something else. If tonight is not about Susana, maybe my soul and I will talk about that other intention: to put a bit more order in my life... Was this the first or the second? *To order your life, you'll first have to disorder it!,* my inner voice cries out, like an command from the Master and a gentle advice from my shark. My soul is answering the question.

Next, I undress

"I Surrender, I Trust, I Accept, and I am Grateful...", I repeat behind my blindfold, seeking to unveil the profound meaning of each of those words, taking refuge in them.

The order to first disorder everything comes from a confident and firm part of me, from my absolute center. It's a resolution. Perhaps that's why it causes so much *fear*, a word which in my mind now holds only one meaning: surrender.

But what does surrender mean in this case? What do I need to disorder? What do I need to unlearn?

The current order of my life is composed of pieces that are not all mine –I think, and nod in agreement–. *There are decisions I've made, desires, traumas, and mandates that don't belong to me.*

This half-own, half-foreign order has brought me here. I'm ready to separate the wheat from the chaff and it's still too hard. It's not just the idea of disorder that terrifies me. It's also not knowing what awaits me. And how does one surrender to disorder?

The air tastes like loss, of a fatal loss. It's as if I'm in the middle of the jungle and right there, in the darkness, the dampness brings me the voracious gaze of the tiger and the snake.

Something hurts a lot, something beyond the skin. My aura hurts. The earth hurts.

The Return of the Shark

The animal emerging from these shadows is not the friendly, kind, wise shark from my first ayahuasca experience in the Sierra de Madrid. While that one was fierce, it was more like a cartoon; this one I see in front of me is real, like in the documentaries; with its imperfect teeth, red and sore gums, fins in attack position.

Unlike that wise shark who didn't want to hurt me "because I've already eaten," this one intends to devour me. It passes by once, twice, three times with its jaws open. And although I resist being swallowed and pierced through, I know I have no choice; I'll have to surrender.

Terrified, I accept my fate. "It's okay, eat me, come on, open your mouth," I say to it. And zigzagging in slow motion, from the shadows of these deep sea depths where there is only dense darkness, the beast's jaws begin to widen. They widen until the horrendous white carnivore devours my entire soul.

By surrendering to that wise shark of my first ayahuasca ceremony, the one that didn't want to eat me, I was taken to a beautiful tunnel and to a higher level.

By letting myself be eaten by this one, the beast takes me into its guts.

Mom's Crying

That May 28th, 1974, the day I was born, could have been sunny or rainy, I don't know. For my mother, it was a bit of both.

Her father (Grandpa José) had been agonizing from cancer for several months. As I've been told, he hadn't died before "just to wait for me to be born." A few days after meeting me in person, he passed away.

For my mother, who likely had a powerful Electra complex (the female equivalent of Oedipus) with her father, her entire pregnancy with me passed hand in hand with agony, which I experienced while growing in her womb. I don't think I'm wrong to feel that it was after his death, her dad's, that my mother began to be consumed by depression.

Now, I'm being devoured by the shark. And the tunnel is neither beautiful nor magical. It's a fleshy tube that, at times, appears to me like the tentacles of an octopus that are sucking me into oblivion. And that tunnel doesn't lead me to another higher plane of the "video game." It takes me inside my mom's womb.

Once there, I observe, like in a flesh-colored ultrasound, the baby I was. While I'm here, with him, sharing that space, I look outside. And I can see my Grandpa José in his agony, being slowly consumed by cancer, staying alive only to meet me. I see my mother who, instead of embracing the joy of life to come, cannot stop grieving for the one leaving. And now, the lack of acceptance envelops me too. These nine months now pass before my covered eyes.

Suddenly I find myself in my grandparents' house (which was now just "grandma's house"), in my mother's arms, climbing some stairs. I watch her from the top floor, climbing the old marble steps one at a time, in sleepy agony. I hear the words that baby is absorbing: "Now that my dad is gone, I only have you, my baby. You're not going to leave me ever. You're mine. You're part of me, a piece of me. Now I only have you. I will never, ever let you go..."

The Echo of the Universe and the first election

The deep understanding of the origin of my sadness finally allows me to continue my journey. Then, that place of Expanded Consciousness, that Ur from which we all come, reappears before me, but in a different way.

I yawn and release a lethargic weight trapped in my chest. And, immediately after, I hear that same sound, my yawn, echoing to my left, in some distant corner of the room. Having caught my attention, I momentarily abandon the ayahuasca dream to refocus my mind, which lies beside me. *Could someone have imitated me?* Curious and amazed, I feign another similar sound, trying not to speak or disturb the other participants, who are resting in their respective dreams.

The echo responds again. And once more. Now it's undoubtable.

Either someone is imitating me or I can't find a logical explanation for this, I whisper to my reason. Then I understand. It's not just any echo; this is the Echo of the Universe. It's a clear manifestation. The one of that wisdom we all know so well: "What one projects into the universe, comes back." It's about the thoughts and actions we send out returning to us; they materialize, shaping our lives. The Echo, then, is one of those deep understandings. I no longer need to put them in a box or highlight them in my mind. They're now so natural that they don't need to be emphasized for anyone; deep down, we all know these truths.

This place where I find myself, where I can access whenever I want, is now filled with sounds and colors. Its infinite walls not only return my sounds and thoughts to me; they return my feelings.

At this precise moment, when I feel a dark fear approaching from a distance, I conduct another experiment. I don't want to feel that fear now, although I know I won't be able to avoid it for long; I want to feel peace. So, I ask the music coming from the speakers to soften. I indicate, with a smile, for it to turn off the drums resonating in the distant darkness of the room. And the music responds to me. It doesn't follow my orders; it obeys other higher patterns that I still don't understand or master. However, as if it wanted to teach me something, it grants me grace for a moment.

The shadowy chords that threatened me moments ago begin to blend into the mist. It dissolves to give way to a radiant melody of inspiration, which now permeates the atmosphere. I understand what's happening, yet I cannot help but be amazed.

I can direct the music –I tell myself–. *I can change my mood. I can change my reality, at will!... Or almost.*

The rehearsal works only for moments. The next fear is still lurking. I am proud of myself; by changing the energy projected towards the Echo of the Universe, I haven't avoided or ignored the fear. It's as if I've said to it: "Not now, please; give me a break." As if I've asked for it, without ignoring its presence, which is already too much. I realize now the difference between escaping from fear and, from my center, *choosing* to project something different into the world.

The fear of homosexuality

In the midst of this beautiful Echo of colors and feelings, returns, like one more, that fear of the imminent. It's as if, still lying in the middle of the jungle, from the darkness of the vines and bushes, the eyes of that tiger were calculating, patiently, the time of its attack. It's that same pain of the aura and the mud. I accept that the next animal awaits me; I don't try to evade it.

But there's no animal or figure. It's just a shapeless sensation; a feeling of anguish like few times I've experienced in life. I'm not short of breath; it's not a panic attack, like other times; it's not an energy that leads me to the pain of my ancestors. It's something absolutely mine. Very dark, too intimate.

I've already known the power to change the music of my surroundings. But that Echo of the Universe, more powerful than me, seems to bring me now another instance of choice. The voice returns, reminding me: "To bring order to your life, you first have to disorder... EVERYTHING."

Faced with the presence of pain, and once again asking myself what I should do, how to surrender to the disorder that scares my soul so much, a clear sensation comes to me. That of something I've hidden for too long; something I still can't decipher within me: the fear of homosexuality.

I don't know if all heterosexual people have homosexual desires or thoughts at some point. I don't want to generalize this as a shield. I've had them, and maybe I still do. I've recognized them many times in my life, that's true. The feminine part, in some way, is assumed in me; but maybe only in the right side of my brain. It embarrasses me and I prefer to hide it. Until now.

That desire, or more precisely the fear of that jungle phantom, is present in my life. I don't know exactly what that fear is. I don't know how to describe it at this point in the ceremony. But the truth is that, in this present moment, while embracing the pain of the aura and the earth, I feel it's time to uncover it. Or that I have to do it if I don't want to delve deeper into the jungle.

Now I understand that with a violent and overprotective mother on one side, and a cowardly and absent father on the other, it would have been logical for me to end up being gay. In that case, it wouldn't have been by choice but rather by conditioning, pushed by the trauma of that maternal-paternal structure. And amidst this colorful Echo of the Universe, I feel a strong empathy with everyone, heterosexual or LGBT+, with all those who choose a sexual identity from their center, from their Inner Being; not because their traumas chose for them.

I feel compassion for those who suffer in silence. I celebrate and admire those who have chosen their sexuality for themselves, whatever it may be. All of this is a step in my own understanding. And yet, it's not enough.

Among the colors and sounds of this beautiful place, I return to my forbidden desire. And I still feel that fear of homosexuality. Like with any other fear, the ayahuasca experience forces me into an imminent step: I must surrender.

But this causes me even more dread. *What does it mean to surrender, in this case? Do I have to materialize homosexuality? Do I have to "suck a dick" to surrender to this fear?!* —And the questions continue—. *What should I do to "let myself be penetrated" by this fear?* Entertaining these possible situations scares me more than the original fear.

Perhaps that's why the answer comes, clearer than ever, to my being. I realize something wonderful: homosexuality is just one more feeling, neither good nor bad. It's just one that I don't choose. At least, not for now.

Unbeknownst to me, that third intention I cast into the universe at the beginning of the ceremony returns reflected in an Echo of colors, like a disordered rainbow.

It has cost me a lot to get here. The terrain has been difficult. But I've come to my first great choice: despite (or even because of) the variety of desires that arise in me, I choose to be heterosexual. I choose my wife, Susana (at least for now), even though I also like other women... And here comes another big decision, one that I still have to face. I sense that this fear of homosexuality, with the divergent forms it's taking, will return, somewhat more relaxed, tonight.

Returning barely to myself, I noticed that sweat has soaked my eye mask. I take it off. I see that "Susana" in front of me; she's sitting on her mat, in a meditation position. She looks at me and nods her head, gently, affirmatively, as if to say: "That's right..."

The scream that dad kept inside

If the unconscious, like the brain, had a left and a right side, I now withdraw from the former, exhausted. It's time to face my father.

When I spoke to him at the previous ceremony, he told me that his pain was "the pain of Man who screams in silence." And I came to this understanding: his absence may have something to do with the pain held back by all the men in my family tree. Now I'm at peace with that, but not with his cowardice and his inability to be present. My father, who I was able to count on in many ways, was not there when I needed him the most: that time when, tired of living with my mother, I went to ask him for a place to stay.

On that occasion, he did receive me, yes. But after a couple of months, he kicked me out of his house.

To make matters worse, he didn't do it directly. He was subtle, manipulative, and cowardly with his words.

Now, in this crawl space of my unconscious, I turn to the right and go looking for him. He's there, inert.

I begin to explain to him how much he hurt me when he asked me to return to my mother's house. But it's not enough.

I decide to take him with me to that day, to that scene, which I now remember perfectly. The smell of leather from that armchair in the living room, where I slept happier than in my room at my mother's house, woke me up every morning. I no longer slept late like my mother. I got up with my father at seven, with the *mate*[2] that he sometimes brought me.

But the morning of this scene is different.

---

[2] *Mate* is a traditional South American tea-like hot drink, particularly popular in Argentina, Uruguay, Paraguay and parts of Brazil.

In the apartment, which has barely one bedroom and a living room, I have much less space and fewer material things. However, inside me, I'm more comfortable, I fit better. And he knows it.
—Look son —he says, preparing for a tender fatherly explanation—. You know I like having you here. We get along well. You behave well. It's a pleasure to have you here. But you also know that I live with Betty, that she's my girlfriend and she's a grown woman... For her to wake up in the mornings and see you, a sixteen-year-old boy, lying on the sofa, isn't nice; neither for her, nor for you.
Something inside me expected these words, even though I don't want them.
—But I'm fine here, dad. I don't mind sleeping on the couch. I'm happy here.

Both my father and I are now watching the scene as if present on the set of a movie.

He continues:
—I know that living with your mom is difficult, but that's your home and one day you will have to go back. I think you've been here long enough, with us; and you can always come back when you need to. Think about it. You don't have to leave now. Take your time. No one is kicking you out...
The boy believes him. The father must be right. After all, the arguments are reasonable.

So, I enter the scene and tell my father, without a trace of bitterness:

—Scream! Shout out what you really want to say, what you feel. Stop spinning your words. Spit it out without cowardice. Let it out already!

I'm the one who has to give him the words.
And someone who I don't remember ever raised his voice or hand to me, now shouts:

—I don't want to take care of you! Don't you get it? I want you to leave my house! Go away! I can't take care of you, I don't want to! I'm sorry, I know you don't want to go back to that crazy batshit woman, but I want to live my life. I want to do whatever the fuck I want! And I don't want to take care of you!

In the next scene, the teenager is alone; maybe a few days later, perhaps moments.

He's leaving his father's house. He turns the doorknob, opens it slowly, looks back.

Everything happens now in slow motion, as if each frame were suspended, slowed down by sadness, a sadness without tears, that the boy does not understand.
For some reason, when I see his face, it's not me. The face is that of my nephew Santiago, who is now eighteen years old. Maybe it's too hard to see my own features; maybe my nephew also needs his teenage pain to be seen. "Santi, I see your pain," I tell myself, I say to him.

Now the boy is opening the elevator doors of the building where his mother lives; where he no longer inhabits.

This scene is also slow. And in each inert pause, we can notice the compulsive movements of a mind that doesn't need to remember.

Like a robot, the teenager closes the elevator doors. He moves them with the same perfection with which he had opened them, seven floors below. With the same resignation, he inserts the key into the top lock, two turns. Then, in the one below, two and a half turns. He doesn't even have to use his gaze, still frozen in his father's scream. There are tears in his eyes.
He breathes through his mouth, with an agitation that doesn't correspond to the physical effort exerted.
As he enters the hallway, he turns his head towards the living room and sees. He sees the obese figure of his mother sleeping in her bed, in that living room where every day, he witnessed her lethargy, extended until late in the afternoon.
Once again, the teenager enters his room. He closes the door slowly, turns the key. Without being tired, he lies down to sleep.

Resting is not the same as sleeping

I am lying with my hands on my chest. These slowed-down scenes allow me to better accept what I experienced in my adolescence. But they also allow me to see things as they were, to call things by their name. I no longer want to justify my father's absence; I no longer want to endure my mother's outbursts of rage.

"But why can't I just vomit all of this out once and for all, get it out of my stomach?" I protest. In neither the first nor the second ceremony have I vomited, despite trying. I've only managed a shout or a yawn, a thread of saliva. And yet, in the ayahuasca, that purge seems to be extremely important.

Someone once told me that she, in her vomit, had expelled all the words of abuse with which her father had drilled her during her childhood. And throughout the night, I try to do it twice. *The third time is the charm*, I think. I lean over the little green bucket. Nothing comes out. I have no food. But I don't even release the water I've been drinking. A lot, as it is consumed here. When I arrived early this afternoon, I offered to help with the preparation of the ceremony. The shaman asked me if I could go buy water, thirty gallons. I needed help from a young man who, like me, had arrived early to choose his spot.

Yawns were enough for me in my first ceremony; wetting myself was my purge in the second. What will it be this time? I'm not going to wet myself again; at least it's not what I choose.

And then I notice that, over the last few hours, I've been sweating profusely. Although it's almost summer, the air conditioning has been maintaining a pleasant temperature all night. *Did the shaman turn off the air conditioning to make us experience the heat?* –I wonder–. *Just as he programs the playlist of music to guide emotions; just as he blows smoke to take us out of our comfort zone, surely he turns off the air conditioning to provoke sweat* –my ego says, emerging from some remote corner of its rest.

But that's not the case. It's already early morning; it must be cold outside. The sweat is mine. The copious drops that are growing on my forehead, and that overflow my skin to then wet my pillow, are absolutely my own. And so exaggerated and continuous that perhaps they are also from my ancestors; from that endless branch of men who paid, for generations, with blood, sweat, and without tears.

Now not one but both of the pillows I brought from home are soaked. I realize that I've been switching them from side to side as they got wet, and then swapping them. Neither the blanket I brought (the one that only our dogs use now) is enough to dry the rivers of sweat, the drops that by this time of night could have filled several glasses.

"When you sleep, you meet your mom," Mauricio's words echo.

It's true. And it's also true that, I've always had a problem with pillows. None are comfortable enough for me, none seem suitable for resting. In the same way, these two I brought don't suffice to absorb all the sweat, all this fatigue (the one that belongs to me and the one that doesn't), all the pain.

I realize that I'm really exhausted. Tired like never before, or maybe aware of it like I've never been. And some words, containing an invincible truth, come out of me: *I want to rest and write, rest and write... Resting is not the same as sleeping.*

Finally, after so many years of needing them to fall asleep, I remove the pillows… to try to rest.

The Vomit of Mom

I'm back in the apartment I shared with my mother and sister; my mother levitating in her restless sleep on the sofa bed in the living room. I wake up to look out the window of my room. I can clearly see the stickers on the glass, the face of the teenager leaning against it, the scraps of the floral wallpaper in my room, which I was removing to write the names of my current girlfriends on the plaster.

"Open!" my mother commands, without any authority. The bear, suspended in her hibernation, knocks on my door with hunger.

—So your dad kicked you out of his house, huh? I already suspected it. Of course, he only cares about his own life, washing his hands of other people's problems. The things your old man has done to me...!

My mother unloads her rage again. No matter the reason, the spark, the excuse; everything ends in shouts, insults, "vomits".

—Can't you see you're just like your father? You disrespect me. You ignore me. That face you make! Just like your father's!

As usual, I perceive the impending slaps of the flip-flop, magnified by the drums of the music coming from the speakers; and suddenly a knife, flying nearby, with enough aim to not hurt my flesh:

—I regret having given birth to you!

Boom! I see, in front of me, on the film of my life projected on the eye mask, my mother's scream turned into an immense vomit, which is suspended in slow motion until it stops completely in the air. It's as if that scream had shape, eyes, hands, pieces. I see it sideways, like in a three-dimensional video game. The remains of vegetables, the pieces of swallowed meat.

And now how do I write all this?

It's clear that the fear of homosexuality, my mother's blows and shouts... all this disorder will have a reason. Something I must put in order.

But the fear now is of a different nature. I embarked on writing a testimony of my ayahuasca ceremonies. I've already narrated the first two experiences, and in them, when I recalled some scenes of my mother's violence, I've already wondered: *How do I write this without my mother reading it and having a fit?*

In her favor, I will say the following. On the one hand, there were many good things for which I am grateful: pushing me to go to therapy (even knowing that it would confront me with her); giving my sister and me the only rooms in the house and staying herself in the living room; at some point, the love for writing; countless moments and learnings. On the other hand, the violence, the beatings (even the episode with the knife, which only happened once) really occurred. Although maybe today, in the narrative, they sound more dramatic than they were; they were different times.

But it's not about the real quantity or intensity. It's about how I, as a child, experienced those incidents. And in that, the drama of the story falls short.

I don't want to be unfair and blame my mother for being a criminal who should go to jail. In some corner of my spirit, I forgive her, if pertinent, since it's possible that we choose our families before being born. But it is important, as an adult, not to justify her actions, which is what one does as a teenager; to call them now by their names, whether they are "abuse," "violence," "vomit," or whatever my heart wants to pronounce tonight.

That said, I am terrified of writing it all; as much as my mother reading my book; as much as revealing my fear of homosexuality. *Fortunately, I don't have to face all of that yet* –I tell myself–. *When the time comes to write, or even to publish... I'll see what I do.* But the fear doesn't go away, and I think that, at some point, I'll be able to talk about it with my mother. And that's when an image appears to me.

I am facing her; we are in a Zoom session (I know it's not very beautiful but that's how it comes up; after all, she lives in Argentina and I in Los Angeles; and although she hasn't spoken to me in a long time, this is how we communicate). She is on the screen, and I say to her:

Mom, I want you to know that I'm going to publish a book. In it, I talk about all the painful things you did to me, and how much they affected my life: the violence, the screams, the knife... You're not going to like it. These won't be pages you proudly show your friends. Maybe it's better if you don't read them. But it's what I'm going to do. And I want to tell you something else: every time we talk, you and I, like right now, there's a glass, like a windshield, between us. In that glass are embedded your screams, your violence, that "I regret having given birth to you," all those words. The good things are there too, of course, but these are the ones that hurt. And I can't look you in the face ignoring that glass. I can, perhaps, set it aside for a few moments (knowing it's there) and talk to you without it interfering with our vision. But I'll never be able to ignore it; not just for me, but to clear the path for those who come after me. I know you yourself suffer from the guilt of those abuses. You don't need to carry that weight anymore. You too can choose for that glass not to define your life.

Even more terrifying than this dialogue with my mother is the issue of homosexuality. I've already processed something a few moments ago, while I was in the Echo of the Universe. But I also don't know if I'll be able to write about this. So I look among my ideas for some creative way to hide it. Maybe, instead of recounting this last ceremony, I can put "Third Chapter: ...", and leave a whole page blank. Or I can even say that "the experience was too intimate; I exercise my right to privacy." I think of a thousand ways not to say it, but... of course, it's the fear of writing. And in the face of fear, if I don't want to perpetuate it, there's only one way out: surrender. Now that I know it, maybe I'll never be able to avoid it.

The Echo of the Universe and the Second Election

Just realizing it was enough for the disordered colors of the rainbow to return. Once again, I find myself in the midst of this infinite space where everything that is projected becomes materialized. The colors come and go, bounce off, mix with the music emanating from the speakers, and the feelings vibrating within me. They are disordered so that, with my creativity, I can mix them as I choose.

Fear, somewhere in this mirage, still lurks among the colors. But it is clearing up: it is the fear of my feminine side. Perhaps of sexuality, energy, joy. *After all, the word gay* –I remind myself– *means "joy"*.

And again: *But what does surrender mean in this case?* I try to find that meaning. My mind is already back on the sidelines, I don't need it; but the question bounces in this space of sensations.

I think of my mother, I know that's where this energy comes from. I think of my father's absence. I think of the blows to the skin, the blows to the heart... My wife Susana and I never hit our daughters. I acknowledge that sometimes we yell at them, that we lose our center, that we are not perfect parents. I confess that more than once I wanted to raise my hand like my mother did to me. Fortunately, that doesn't cross the barrier of my mind.

But now I think of the two puppies we adopted at home, whose blanket "coincidentally" covers me. My daughters could have given them some strong, masculine names, perhaps Thor for the male, and for the female, some empowered woman's name from a movie. Instead, they named them Cookie and Brownie. More feminine, impossible.

At this moment, with the image of my mother's blows, comes the image of the two puppies. But it's not the sweet image of their faces, one brown, the other black. It's the one when they've broken dozens of things at home, and which to this day add up to hundreds of dollars.

When that happened, at first, my immediate reaction was to grab a flip-flop and want to hit them. Hatred came from the depths of me and nothing could stop it. I knew it was wrong. So, before delivering the blow, Susana tried to convince me not to hit them. The girls hugged the dogs to protect them from my fury. It was this image, that slap of shame, that made me come to my senses. And I don't hit them. Sometimes I'm very close to doing it; other times I aim at the floor, just to scare them with the snap (like my mother aimed the knife elsewhere), although in my mind I do punish them with fury. With the same fury my mother used; with the same anger with which, now, she appears before me, flip-flop in hand.

I assimilate that image with mine, slapping the poor puppies. I don't know if it's shame, pain, memory, reflection. Something in this Echo of the Universe brings me that image and returns to me, in the form of a concept, the answer: "Cookie and Brownie are the beasts of creativity that want to break everything!"

The fear of creativity

That's it; the fear of creativity. And another "Ah... Of Course!" descends upon my understanding. All the answers come down at once: *The puppies represent the repressed creative impulse, my feminine side, writing, my creativity that I want to silence with blows because it scares me.*

The decision to adopt Cookie and Brownie was neither easy nor planned. For years the girls insisted they wanted a dog, and Susana and I refused. It's not relevant to remember the details, but the reality is that one morning we went to visit an animal shelter with the intention (not even the decision) of seeing cats. And we came back home with something else. There, in the shelter, where there were only dozens of large, old, barking dogs, two puppies were waiting for us in one of the glass-enclosed rooms. We asked about them, thinking they were already taken. To our surprise, the caregiver's response was: "No, they're here for people to meet them and adopt them." "And are there more puppies?" we insisted. "No, they're the only ones. And I don't want to rush you to take them; I'm not a car salesman," said the caregiver, sincerely. "But if you don't take them, someone else will in fifteen minutes."

We thought about it for a few seconds; I didn't trust that it was true. And although we hadn't yet gone through the entire kennel, we decided to say yes, that we would adopt them; after all, while the paperwork was being processed, we could think it over.

That's how, by choice or destiny, we ended up with two dogs at home. Susana and I were so scared by our hasty decision that we felt invaded, deceived. And we decided to return them the next day. To cut a long story short, the shelter in downtown Los Angeles made it so difficult for us to return them that we ended up keeping them. In the end, we had accepted the situation. But just like now in this ayahuasca memory, the dogs came with pain, with fear; with that fear with which creativity bursts forth to disrupt, to destroy everything before creating order.

Now I see it clearly. "Cookie and Brownie are the beasts of creativity that want to break everything!" And, I repeat, they've broken everything; especially, very especially, four pairs of flip-flops that I continue to buy and rebuy, without understanding why.

Now I understand. Both Susana and I are currently in a creative process, which both satisfies us and separates us from each other. It breaks us inside and orders us. Susana, with her songs and her *"Ya me cuido yo"*[3], is creating from her masculine energy, from her Cookie. I, with my writing, am discovering the fear of my Brownie, the female puppy.

It's very clear, but it's also scary. And it's because of that fear of creativity that wants to break through, burst forth from the heart, that I've been beating it down with flip-flops; just like my mother did with me.

---

[3] Translated "I'll take care of myself", this is the name of one of Susana's songs, which I recommend to listen to.

No more. From now on, when my puppies break something, when my inner child wants to express his creativity, I won't hit them with flip-flops. I'll look at them with a smile. I choose to let my creativity out.

Efrén wants to fly

Just three days ago, I was writing an article about an interview I conducted with Efrén Ramírez, a Latino actor who had a small role in the Disney-Pixar movie, *Lightyear*, the prequel to *Toy Story*. In it, I mention that Efrén plays the role of a crew assistant; from the base, on the ground, he helps Buzz Lightyear (the main character) fulfill his mission to fly at hyperspeed and save his own. However, the message of my news piece is a bit deeper: Efrén's great career in film and television in Hollywood barely allowed him to play a small role (a couple of lines of script) in a huge blockbuster like *Toy Story*. I say that he is proud of it, but that it shows how difficult it is to be in a big Disney movie, even for actors with a career already established in the industry. I wasn't satisfied with that article. And ayahuasca reveals to me why.

I had just started writing the article when I felt... something. In fact, it was during the interview that I experienced it, and when I sat down in front of the computer, I wrote: "Efrén wants to fly."

That wasn't the final title. The actor hadn't given me that answer, and while you change one word or two to embellish the piece, it's important to stay true to journalistic work and to the concepts expressed. But what I felt was very strong, very clear. Efrén doesn't want to be a runway assistant; he wants to be a pilot! And as grateful as he may be for Disney including a

Latino character to "fill the diversity box," as humble as he must show himself (and he surely is), Efrén wants to fly!

That's what I perceived from his soul. Maybe because it's the same thing I feel in mine. Just like Efrén, I want to be the pilot of my ship, the ship of my creativity. I also want to fly. As for hyperspeed... I don't know yet.

The other meaning of smoke

At some point before this encounter, I told Iván, the shaman, that during the two previous ceremonies –the first in Madrid with another shaman, and the second with him, last year–, the issue of smoke had affected me very badly during the experience.

"When they exhale smoke on me, my breath is cut off and I end up in a panic attack, as if I couldn't breathe," I said, hinting that, please, this time don't come close to throw smoke at me during the ceremony. He didn't let me finish speaking and replied with a smile: "This time, perhaps, smoke will have another meaning for you."

Once again, I was trying, unsuccessfully, to manipulate the experience.

Now, between the endless threads of sweat and the replacement of one pillow for another, I feel the urge to urinate. It's the second or third time I've done it tonight. The smoke fills the room, but I've barely noticed it. With difficulty, I get up. Even harder, I walk towards the arch on the right, which leads to the bathroom. I look for someone to accompany me. No one is paying attention to me. So I continue. I walk slowly, so as not to fall.

Why would I need help? I just have to walk slowly. How do the elderly do it, then, when they don't have anyone around? They walk slowly, leaning on a railing to support themselves. I am my own support. I am my own path. I just have to slow down, I think in silence.

I help myself with the bars as I pass by the stairs. I hold onto the railing to climb the two small steps that lead me to the next level of the floor. I see the small anteroom I have to go through, and there are Iván and another guy. Iván has tribal makeup on his face and wears a headdress of feathers. Like his companion, his bare torso is adorned with tattoos. Both are in the middle of their own smoke ritual.

The shaman sees me coming. He notices the difficulty in my steps but doesn't extend his hand to me. He just looks at me. As I approach them, the thick smoke envelops me too. This frightens me, I feel like I won't be able to breathe. When I'm about to continue on to the bathroom, Iván does offer me his hand.

There are no words. I just know I have to breathe deeply, that I have to breathe in the smoke, let it pass through me and out, as if it were a cool breeze. I try. I think of my father, smoking one or two packs of cigarettes a day until he was hospitalized with a pre-heart attack. I think of his death, of the apnea that blows through me at night, and when I want to realize it, I'm breathing in the smoke in naturally deep breaths; I inhale and exhale the smoke through me. I no longer feel fear in my lungs; I breathe as if I were letting fresh air pass through them.

After a few minutes, the smoke turns into smoke. I begin to feel the normal and common discomfort of the situation. My bladder reminds me of the reason I'm here. And I continue, with the gait of an elderly person, through the labyrinth that leads me to the bathroom.

While I'm emptying the yellow tears, I notice that second candle I had added when I first entered this room. Its glow dazzles me.

This afternoon I had thought that one candle wouldn't be enough. Now I turn off the extra one. *One light was enough*, I tell myself with an upside-down smile.

And I head towards the garden.

The reflection of death is...

The garden of the house is nearly deserted, contrasting deeply yet uncertainly with the interior. Apart from some soul seated on a wicker sofa, everything is solitude and breeze. I look up at the sky, as if searching for the stars, the ancient drawing of the zodiac. It's a cloudy and quiet night. The moon is not visible. Except for the chirping of crickets, everything is silence; a silence not broken by giant vomits or cotton yawns.

Everything seems normal until I lower my gaze to the grass. It is divided into two zones, non-existent during the afternoon. One part is green, normal, but in the other, larger one, the surface is gray. At first it seems like dry grass, but then I see that it's not, that it's really ash gray, as if recently devoured by fire.

I am fully aware of what is happening around me. Sometimes something seems different to me but immediately, when I focus my mind, it reveals itself for what it is. Behind a plant, for example, I just saw a large lump move like a bear; upon noticing it, I discovered it was one of the participants, walking around with a poncho. But the grass is gray, it is ash. I wonder if that object in the middle is some kind of smoke machine, placed there to create a sort of graveyard, as is often done on Halloween nights. But no, there is no such device, and yet no matter how much I focus my sight, the grass remains as quick ash.

Just in case, I decide to stay in the green area. I sit down. I take a deep breath and then rest my head on the cool grass. I am proud to be completely relaxed, resting; not needing any pillow.

But the gray grass is still there. I almost feel like it's getting closer to me, gaining ground. It's not possible. There is a perfect, straight line that delimits both spaces, the green and the ashy. And I'm not crazy.

Once again, anticipating that fear may arise, I think: *I have to surrender, before the graves of my ancestors appear... or something worse.*

Slowly, I crawl like a snail, and I approach, stealthy, to the border of the green. Carefully, I touch the gray. And nothing happens. It's grass, I can confirm it. But it's gray!

I stand up, close my eyes. Before taking the step forward, to the other side, the memory of the ceremony held in Topanga Canyon briefly comes to mind when, on that garden soil, like this one, I suffered a panic attack; when unable to breathe the fresh air and fearing to enter where the smoke was, I felt surrendering meant touching my feet and descending through the roots of the Pachamama, to the suffering of all my ancestors.

Now, as I finally surrender to the gray earth and step on it wholeheartedly, I look up. I smile, and what bathes me is a silver glow. The reflection of death was simply the moonlight that, projected, painted that segment of the grass gray! The moon does not have its own light, like the sun. It only reflects that of the sun. I, like her, project my light to the Echo of the Universe.

I sit again on the grass. It no longer looks gray. I lie down. I breathe. No. I don't need a pillow. "You only need the earth." I raise my hands, impose them towards the celestial body, as defense, as one who accepts to give and receive its light, as one who sets limits to the moon.

The Echo of the Universe and the third choice

I walk back, slowly and consciously, to the living room, to my bed. The gravity of my head hollows the pillow. The silver bottle is still there, next to the travel journal; the pencil prevents it from closing completely, as if giving freedom to the last words.

I anticipate the melodies of the night again. If pain comes, I don't avoid it, I look it in the eyes, to then project happiness to the Echo of the Universe. And in the midst of this joy, I feel like writing it all down. There are too many teachings from this night to let them slip away. I don't want any detail to be lost in the smoke of oblivion.

As in the previous ceremony, my anxiety tells me: *If I write, I can't live it; if I live it, I fear not remembering.* But now the unease is even worse. The teachings and revelations are scattered in this Echo of the Universe, in different energy planes, with shapes and colors that connect.

I know another message is coming, I sense it.

I feel the sweat on my forehead, on my chest again. It's so much water that my body loses that I fear dehydration and dying again. But the liquid in my bottle has absorbed the vibrations of the fears of those in this room; it is charged with their pain and joys. So, I don't drink it, for fear of swallowing all those vibrations. I know that, even though I have sweated, the body can live with little water. I don't need to drink. But I do need to write all this down, lest I forget it.

Don't write now —my conscience tells me—. Stay calm. All the revelations of tonight are just dis-ordered. The moment will come when you can integrate it all. But now let them go, don't be afraid of losing them. Later, the feminine energy will come to help you re-order, hand in hand with creativity!, by the choice of your absolute center! Now, you just have to live it.

I remember that creativity is taking two or more unrelated things and combining them in a way that something new emerges. I deeply understand what the fears in the middle of the Echo of the Universe have been for.
One can only create when there is disorder.
Only from chaos does a new order arise. To recombine the pieces floating in that chaos, *creativity* is needed.
Now I understand why those three initial intentions (putting order in my life, acting from the 'adult', having a fuller relationship with Susana), appeared disordered, overlapping, among the fears of the night. It was to let me release my feminine energy, and thus, help me reorder. "To order my life, first I have to disorder it." I am ready for the new paradigm, for this new order that, this time, I will knead according to my choice, from my center.

Choosing from the Adult, the True... Third Choice

Once again, although the teachings are as clear as water and fear is asleep, the question is: "What does surrendering to my choice mean at this moment?" I review in my mind the fears and understandings of this night, deep rivers in which choice has been the current to guide their channels. Some had an undecided course, others ran underground. Creativity is energy, untamed. Choice is the only thing in my power. After all, all those fears, like rivers, will flow into the sea.

As a gateway, the fear of disorder has manifested itself to me and everything I must work on before focusing on improving the relationship with my wife: those conflicts with my mother and father that, like ghosts of the house, roam the basement of my unconscious.

At the same time, in that first Echo of the Universe, the fear of homosexuality appeared. But I understood that this is nothing but another feeling, one that I do not choose now.

Then, that same fear has returned with more force to show me that, once surrendered to my feminine side, it was creativity that wanted to come out and break everything; the same one that I repressed, like my puppies, with flip-flop in hand.

And in this clarity that begins to take shape, the third choice emerges; perhaps the most important and around which this whole experience has revolved. *Choosing* in itself.

It is the choice itself. That of my present, of now: choice as the origin of everything, regardless of what I am choosing.

What do I do tomorrow?

I came to this ceremony not with determination, but with an open mind and willingness to stay for both nights, to partake the four plant intakes —two of ayahuasca and two of San Pedrito, twice each. But now, the ghost of caution returns to me.

Like a year ago, two sensations struggle within me: I want to continue floating in the sea of knowledge and at the same time, I feel satisfied on this shore of my river. Not only do I want to, I know that if I take San Pedrito in the morning, I will intensify all this knowledge; all these understandings will merge with the experiences of others; perhaps I will write wonderful things. Like in my second experience, connected in that way with the universe, I know that my heart will merge with it, in another Family Constellation. I know that path. How could I not desire something so beautiful!

I also know that if I stay for the second ayahuasca, the fears of this night may deepen, but I am also convinced, from my experience, that my rivers will delve even deeper into the amazing sea of understanding, and all pain will have been worth it.

However, this time I realize that those two contradictory sensations, the desire to know more and the satisfaction of having come this far, no longer fight as they did in the second ceremony. Continuing with the other plants not only excites me, but it no longer scares me. I think about how useful it will be, not only for my personal growth, but for the book I am writing, to experience what is coming. And I remember some words from Iván at the beginning of the ceremony:

What most people experience on the second day is the return of the same themes from the first; but this time, to reach a kind of conclusion. That's why, for those who are not sure about staying for both nights, because what they have experienced has been very deep, I tell them to try, precisely for this reason. After the first night, they will think they have worked out what they came to work on. But what awaits them in the second ceremony will be, in general, the completion of that fear, trauma, or issue that came out in the first.

And yet, staying in *this* stage, having come this far, weighs more within me.
So, what do I do tomorrow? Do I take more plants?, I ask, without thinking, to my Inner Self.
I don't want to!, it responds. And in some magical way, I feel that voice coming from my own center. I don't understand. Just this time, when I'm open and eager, less afraid to continue and complete the two days, eager to connect with the universe to write more and better; just now, caution returns, my conservative self... And I'm a little disappointed in myself.

Between wanting and desiring...

With ayahuasca still in my veins and aura, I begin to debate the arguments for and against taking more beyond tonight.
On one hand, the shaman says that the ceremony is planned for two days and four doses, and my desires and experience confirm it, not to mention my commitment "to surrender", "to trust".
But another argument seems to prevail. If two are better than one, and four better than two, then a hundred

are better than four, and a thousand... Where does this end? Even with the full awareness that more doses will result in a greater connection with the Source, more wisdom, more healing, how much is enough? How much of the good is too much? When does the connection to that place from which we come end?

It ends where I decide it ends. It ends with my choice, a wise authority resonates within me.

And another image comes back to me: that of that Pac-Man video game; on a screen, four pills that allow us to eat the ghosts. Like those "clues" we talked about in the second ceremony, these pills allow us to advance in the game and move on to the next level. But what would happen if, instead of four, there were dozens or hundreds of pills that allowed us to eat ghosts? Would the game still be fun? Would it be worth continuing to play?

This image appears to me as a powerful argument to support the decision of my center. It is not an absolute truth or an example for everyone; there will be people for whom twenty or thirty ayahuasca sessions in a year are equivalent to a single Pac-Man pill. But not for me. This is what I choose now. I could and would like to continue connected to my Inner Wise Sage, to everyone around me, and to the universe, in this very direct way. This is a valid and healthy *desire*. But I don't *want* to do it. And now I understand, more than ever, that difference.

Because I also *desire* to eat compulsively. But I don't *want* to do it. In that case, I do it because my addiction is there; my mother is in the food, and it will take me time to overcome it. I *desire* to sleep, but I don't rest. Just like homosexuality is just another feeling and it can even appear as a desire, it's something I don't want. I don't want it from the core of my being; therefore, I don't choose it, just as I don't choose to take San Pedrito tomorrow, and ayahuasca again tonight, and the second San Pedrito on Sunday, even though all of that attracts me and could very well be another valid experience. My inner self tells me I don't want it. I don't want to take more. I desire the sensation of being connected, which will surely come to my writing when I'm in contact with Everything, with everyone (as in that Family Constellation in the universe of the second experience). I'm even certain that would make me learn more. But how far do I want to go? I want to go this far.

The Choice is the Path, and I Choose to Play

If with this first night of revelations I am unleashing my creativity, I don't want to take three more plants that will make me pull everything out at once, go beyond. It may sound mediocre; maybe I need this mediocrity. Somewhere inside me, I fear that creativity will come out so much that I'll spend eighteen hours a day writing and lose time with my family... But deep down, I know it's a healthy fear. I want to keep discovering, keep learning little by little, like in my therapy, week by week. After all, how does a child grow? Occasionally they have a growth spurt, it's true. Perhaps that's what ayahuasca is for me. But before and after that quantum leap, growth occurs gradually, without one perceiving it. Once again, this is my measure. For others, a "growth spurt" might mean a hundred and twenty doses of ayahuasca or who knows what other experiences. In my case (as numerologist Manuel and the elderly Ascension told me), if I have the energy of the master, what would I aim for by continuing to take more plants this weekend? To ascend to the ethereal realm of absolute certainties, to the arrogance of believing that I understand universal truths? No, I don't want that. I don't want to be a master who lives in the sensation of ayahuasca, no matter how pure and true it is. I feel that if I continue with the plan of this ceremony, the energy of the master will be unleashed in its maximum power, and that would be death on this plane.

I don't want to give lectures around the world. As long as I'm on this plane, I just want to be the master of my life, of myself, of my daughters, of what I can teach through my actions, writing, and communication, of the creativity that is emerging, and that I don't want to unleash all at once. I want to keep growing gradually. According to my stars (Gemini with Gemini rising), I am pure mind. Where would my powerful mind end up if I follow the shaman's plan tomorrow and the day after, no matter how perfect it may be? Despite the happiness that ayahuasca still brings to my veins, I fear going to another plane. I want, yes, to experience the feeling of looking in the mirror and seeing that I have "had another growth spurt, and another one..." But I choose this plane. I like this dimension of the soul, where I can play with my daughters, grow with Susana, and enjoy the journey.

Isn't that, perhaps, the only true free will? The choice to play the game of life, or not to play it. I enjoy the advantages that two or three pills on this Pac-Man screen can give me, yes; as long as I know how to take advantage of them. However, as beautiful as it feels to be in contact with the Source, we are in the game for a reason. And after all... I choose to play.

I want to keep learning, little by little. I don't want, for now, more "Profound Understandings" that overwhelm me, that wake me up abruptly. Because it's not just one more night, just one more plant. Knowledge is infinite, and the important thing is not to arrive first; the important thing is the path, the game, life.

Even wanting to take the next plants; even knowing that this is good for me, in this present moment, I clearly understand the meaning of this Third Choice. At least tonight, even more important than the benefit of continuing to take ayahuasca, than everything I can write or connect... is the fact of choosing.

If I know that I choose from my wise adult, if I feel that it is the adult "father" within me who chooses, then "what" I am choosing is just a preference, a something. If desire or impulse is the cause, and carrying it out or not is the consequence, then what is in between is the **action** of choosing from my center. That is, somehow, the path.

And, I repeat to myself, it is the path that matters.

And now, how do I tell the shaman?

The choice and decision, so clear within me, now confront the memory of other words from Iván. He had spoken them before the first ceremony with him (the second for me), in Topanga Canyon. At that time, I hesitated to do two nights of ayahuasca, and even to take the ancient cactus, and he said to me: "The ceremony and the brew that I prepare are set up like a complete program. Depending on the case, sometimes I accept that someone only stays for one night. However, I do not allow skipping the San Pedrito the next day, because it would lose the spirit of the experience and disrupt the connection of the group."

That's why now, in my dialogue with the plant, I even consider the possibility of not talking to Iván and simply pouring the San Pedrito glass behind some plant in the garden; lying, just to avoid having to leave this house. But that would not be honest to him or to myself; nor to what I have been discovering.

By not partaking, in a way, I am about to become the axis of all disorder in this house. But my own axis is so ordered that I not only know what I am going to say to the shaman. I also know that, by doing so, I *choose* the consequences.

Despite my certainty, I still have to confront the person who invited me to this house, to share with these pleasant people. So I rehearse the words in my mind, over and over again.

First, I think of a long speech. Something like: "Look, Iván, last night I had a journey to the depths of my being and from there emerged a certainty. As a consequence, I am not going to take San Pedrito now. And I am not going to take more ayahuasca this weekend either. I have thought about it a lot, but for the first time, I feel that this is a decision that arises from my center, from my Inner Being. I do want to continue feeling the effect of the plant, but I believe that, in this case, the choice is more important than my desire. And that choice is not to continue with another dose of ayahuasca. Still, I would like to stay in this house."

I prepare my defenses to argue, to fight, in case Iván tries to convince me with counterarguments, gets offended, or even tries to manipulate me with his words (*like my father did*, I almost think).

I am ready to say to him: "If four are better than two, who says that a thousand are not better than four...? This is my choice and I accept the consequences of having to leave. If I can stay, without taking more plants, I'll stay. Otherwise, I'll leave, happy."

Whether I stay or leave, I will be proud because that will be the consequence of being the adult "father" of my inner child. "This is my choice," I prepare to assert to Iván, as an irrefutable argument. And so the night goes by.

A new sense of smoke

Someone wakes me up. It's morning, around seven, I imagine, as the sacred cactus ceremony is being prepared. I review the arguments rehearsed during the night. And I am resolved like never before to accept the consequences; the most probable one, having to leave. I am going to express to Iván my desire to stay. But a decision to the contrary will not affect me; I feel, like never before, that I am my own home.

Iván is busy. I intercept him somewhere in the kitchen. Before I can speak to him, he asks me if I can help him carry the plastic cups containing the cactus powder, the next plant, Father. I help him, but finally gather my strength.

—Iván, before San Pedrito, I have something to tell you.

He stops as if to listen to me standing up.

—No. Let's sit down for a few minutes, I'll be brief —I ask with some apprehension, perhaps with embarrassment.

We sit on the edge of two kitchen stools. And these words come out of my heart:

— Iván, you're not going to like what I'm going to say. We don't have time for me to tell you all about last night's experience. But the conclusion is that I'm not going to take any more plants.

—Not even San Pedrito?

—No, not even that. I thought a lot about how to tell you this, and it's hard for me to do. But it's a choice I've made from my center. I also want to tell you that I want to stay all weekend. But I'll understand perfectly if you tell me I can't because I would be in a different vibration than the group.

I finish my speech and wait for a tender argument from him; that I should think it over, that taking more will complete my experience, etc. Or, perhaps, that I have to leave the house. But Iván looks at me and says:
—That's fine. It's your decision. What I was going to ask you is if, even though you're not taking more, you can, please stay.

I hug him, I thank him. And in the midst of my deep emotion, I realize that, unplanned, without thinking about it, Iván is doing what my dad didn't have the courage to do. When I was sixteen, dad manipulated me to kick me out of the house. Now, minutes before the "Father" ceremony, despite my conditions and my firm acceptance of eventually having to leave, Iván is asking me, with love, to stay at his house.

Now, this is finding another meaning to the smoke!

Attraction and choice

There's a girl (there's always a girl, isn't there? However, this is not common in ayahuasca ceremonies). And I'm not referring to the Susan sitting in front of me. It's another girl.

Since I arrived yesterday afternoon at this house, Morgan's green eyes have captivated me. She's young, stunningly beautiful, with blond wavy hair. But what attracts me most about her is her undeniable sensuality. On several occasions, I noticed her looking at me with interest. Yesterday, at some point in the afternoon, we exchanged a few words. I learned that she's a singer and comes from New York.

From some of her comments and gestures, I sensed a kind of sexual energy between us, a sort of magnetism. Later, from a corner of the garden, she looked at me again. I felt she desired me, and that ignited my desire.

But all of that was before the ayahuasca. During the night, I had no contact with her. Honestly, I even forgot about her presence. And now, before the San Pedrito ceremony begins, I feel the weight of her emerald gaze from across the room.

It's time for the sharing circle, where everyone shares their experience from the previous night. After finishing their turn, each person chooses the next one to give their testimony.

Morgan says she had come to work on something related to her sexuality. The missing drop to overflow the glass of eroticism! Now, inside me, I know that if I seek her, I can find her; and that with both of us under the influence of the sacred cactus, achieving a more intimate connection wouldn't be difficult.

But I also remember last night's lesson: "Desiring is not the same as wanting."

I can't help but desire her. But when one desires something and pursues it, one can find it; and one must be willing to accept the consequences. In this case, I know that I do not choose the fact or the consequence of being unfaithful to my wife, Susana. If I really search within myself, beyond the sexual desire of this moment, what do I truly *want*? I want to be faithful to Susana.

I don't deny that, at this moment, I *desire* to be unfaithful. And if the situation were to come towards me, maybe, almost certainly, I wouldn't be able to avoid it. But I choose my wife.

Still, something in me insists on convincing me to change my decision and take San Pedrito. My mind tries one last trick and tells me: *You already chose from your center, not to take San Pedrito. You spoke with Iván; it's done. Now you can choose, from your center, the opposite, and experience Morgan's sensuality intensely.*

Whether it's a real possibility or not, this temptation is too strong. If I let myself be guided by my mind or my instincts, I could even say that I should "surrender" to my desires. But last night's lesson about desiring and choosing is too powerful, too important to set aside.

In reality, I think, this is like a Fourth Choice. Once again, I deeply feel that, even in this case, choosing is more important than the choice itself. It's not about repression; it's about what the "adult" inside me chooses.

Despite the temptations, I stand firm in not drinking from the bowl of San Pedrito or from the forbidden fruit. The first one is easier for me. The second, I sense, will be a struggle throughout the weekend.

All I can do is take more or less voluntary steps to ensure that nothing too intimate happens between Morgan and me.

It's my turn in the sharing circle. While others speak, I ponder what was the most important thing I experienced last night, so I can share with the group; and how to do it briefly. Several transcendent moments, several teachings from "Grandmother" come to mind.

When my turn comes, I notice the "Susan" sitting in front of me, and I spontaneously say to everyone, "Last night, I thought I was coming to work on having a fuller relationship with my wife. But the plant, or something inside me, told me: "Before working on the relationship with Susana, you're going to have to see a couple of things..." And it took me on a journey into the depths of my subconscious, through childhood and adolescence traumas: my mother's depression when giving birth to me; when my father kicked me out of his house..."

As I speak, Morgan looks at me, as attentively as I did during her turn in the round. And precisely when I mention that my intention last night had been "to have a fuller relationship with my wife," her gaze falls to the floor. She makes a gesture of clear disappointment, as if a plan had just been thwarted.

I finish sharing my experience, choose the "Susan" sitting in front of me to share hers, and prepare to engrave her words in my mind:

My intention last night –she begins– *was to work on my relationship with my husband. So far, I've been looking a lot inward, and it's time to look at others; and, above all, at my husband. Last night was beautiful. I saw us together, on the couch, hugging; and lately, I feel like we're losing intensity in our relationship.*

I hoped for some coincidence, but honestly, not this much. The words of this "Susan" seem copied from the ones I just shared.

Now, I think I would have liked to record her, as I fear it might seem made up by me. I know that when I tell Susana, she'll believe me. But I would like to have the recording of what "this Susan" said. This way, it would be clearer how ayahuasca brings out from us the threads that connect us to others; how we can see that these threads join and intertwine in the stream of life, like communicating vessels.

While I hurry to write down Susan's words in my notebook, I feel such a beautiful intrigue that I intend to speak to her as soon as possible, to learn more. I'll try, later, to find the right moment.

The vocational nurse

They must all be under the influence of San Pedrito by now. Everyone, except for me.

I remember my experience from a year ago. By this time in the morning, I was already connecting, soul to soul, with that teenager who, like me, suffered from the absence of her father. Or with those other two young people who reflected, like mirrored silhouettes, part of my own experience at that age.

I also remembered Mauricio's poncho and all those "coincidences"; all those connections that, from time to time, become visible in everyday life. They are those fleeting moments when one cannot believe such a degree of "coincidence". Encountering someone in the most unexpected place, for example. Those unsuspected intersections appear as tips of icebergs; they hide from our short human sight that ninety percent of mass hidden under the sea.

This is how I feel, a bit; as if I only see one end, while others talk among themselves around me. It's interesting to see them from this perspective, from my everyday self. Some are living a slightly more intense experience; lying on their mat, they expel some pain with cries. But most of them act almost "normally".

I see a group of three over there, sitting, chatting with each other as if coming out of a yoga class. Others are helping Nicole, the chef, prepare what promises to be a delicious vegan lunch. It seems like a gathering of friends on any given Saturday, only they're probably not talking about football or finances, but sharing their ayahuasca experiences from last night, finding deep connections, those of the underground roots that unite us all to Pachamama.

But, this time, I don't see just the tip of the iceberg. The physical-chemical effect of the ayahuasca still inhabits me. Perhaps thanks to my choice to stay to rest and write, I perceive a little more than just the visible part of the iceberg.

There is an older woman, about seventy years old, whom I had been observing a while ago. She seems experienced, kind, and tender, but at the same time, she's in control of the situation. At some point, she introduced herself as a "mother-nurse." Then I didn't see her almost all morning. I thought that was her role; to help others. I feel like talking to her, but I see her, precisely, busy with others, with those who need her the most.

She's sitting on the ground now. I approach, a little shy because of her confident attitude, but at the same time, admiring her sense of service. I hope to connect with her; to find that thread of energy that surely binds us.

As soon as we exchange a few words, we find a small coincidence: her father's name was George, the English equivalent of Jorge, my father's name. I narrate to her my almost complete experience from last night, as time is not a concern for us. And in doing so, I get excited about what I've learned in these hours.

She tells me her whole life, her suffering, her family tragedies. I listen to her attentively, with interest. She tells me, among other things, that she's a retired nurse, that she abandoned her profession many years ago, more by choice than by age. Megan is a genuine healer, by vocation. As a nurse, she talked to her patients about their lives, listened to them with interest. She was against giving them more drugs than they needed, and that's why she couldn't beat the Western medicine system.

After more than an hour, despite enjoying our conversation, I still don't find those threads of energy connecting me to her soul; I can't see them in this state foreign to hers, although I still feel proud to have chosen it.

Towards the end of our dialogue, Megan tells me, "Gerardo, you're the person with the highest vibration in this group." I don't know if that's true. It's probably true for her; I must be the only one who has listened to her for so long, the only one who has helped her, the mother-nurse in this hospital of souls.

As I say goodbye, I notice that we were sitting in the garden, right on the grass, then gray, where the moon was reflected last night.

A Mirror of My Anger

The lunch, laid out on the ground as in last year's ceremony, offers a feast of dishes conceived by Nicole, who is in turn an exquisite shaman. This time, I eat neither as little as before nor as much as I would usually in front of such a banquet. Today, the topic of food is not significant to me; it's not about my addictions.

But yes, once again, I understand that one thing is the *desire* to overeat, and another is *wanting* to eat, consciously. I reflect that diets (like the ketogenic one, with pure meat and almond flour pastries) have more to do with **suppressing** the desire to overeat than with *deciding* not to do it.

I used to say that "Keto" was not a diet but rather a way of eating... But the truth is, I don't think it's healthy in the long run.

I argue that, in general, these regimens are a way of suppressing an impulse. Therefore, as statistics prove, more than 90% of people return, after one or two years, to the original weight they had before starting the diet, or even higher. I've witnessed this phenomenon in myself a couple of times.

Now I'm more aware of the difference between desiring and wanting (choosing), which was the great learning from this ceremony. And I complete it with a reflection: when I diet, repressing an impulse (to overeat), it's the child who wants to eat, and the teenager inside me who suppresses it. Instead, when I eat moderately, or avoid eating something I desire but know is bad for me, I'm **not repressing**. What I'm doing is **assuming the strength** to not follow that impulse. It's in these moments, when the adult inside me decides, my center. It's, in a way, choosing what I want, and wanting what I choose.

Suddenly, behind my thoughts, I perceive a hoarse voice saying, "I only eat read meat... pounds of beef. I tried eating vegetables and stuff for a while, but the blood tests were bad. And when I eat only meat, all values are perfect."

I turn around and find Travis's face, whom I briefly met yesterday. He's a big, bald man, with bulging and bloodshot eyes. Before the ayahuasca, he told me something about his anger problem; something I didn't pay much attention to at the time. When I saw him, he reminded me of one of those gangsters from a movie in some maximum-security prison. He just lacked the tattoos covering his skin. I remember thinking: *I hope this guy isn't near me tonight; lest he unleash his anger with the ayahuasca and decides to kill someone.* But luckily, it didn't happen.

Unconsciously, I'm already part of the conversation. Travis talks to two women, probably vegetarians. They seem scared, or at least, disgusted by the words of that "caveman". Travis now addresses me. And before his theory of carnivorousness concludes, the two women have left. They took the opportunity to withdraw from the impromptu group.

I confess I have no desire to listen to him. His energy is so low it weighs; it weighs more than his arguments. Noticing that the women, somewhat offended, have left, Travis comments, "I don't know why they get offended. I, eating meat all day, am strong and healthy. In contrast, she (referring to one of the girls) is a vegetarian, and look how fat she is." I gesture disapprovingly; I feel secondhand embarrassment, perhaps even a little of my own.

Although our conversation is not transcendental (at least not as much as it would have been with San Pedrito's help), it is quite profound. It exposes, among other things, that Travis is a reflection of part of my shadow: anger. Through his words, I learn that within this muscular and fearsome giant, there is a child too wounded, even more than mine; wounded also in the flesh, as his father used to beat him terribly. At one point, and unaware of my experience, he tells me that his father abandoned him at fourteen! And again, I'm amazed by the "coincidence". It's like facing a very dark version of myself, in its pure state.

Despite his brutal and primitive appearance, Travis is, like me, an excellent arguer, and he uses that quality perfectly, with the purpose of sustaining his denial.

He's a skillful lawyer who strives to win a case against himself! In this, he perfectly reflects some of my therapy sessions, where instead of surrendering to Mauricio's advice, I argue over and over again; I fight, I fight, I fight, as if trying to exhaust all possible angles before giving in.

So, entering his game, I tell him:

Travis, I want you to understand that if you feel as bad as you say you do, and you've already tried all possible solutions, as you also say you have, what's good for you is to have weekly therapy. You've already tried the short paths, those medical treatments with antidepressants and such. It would be good for you to now take the long road. And so, little by little, you'll solve your problems. We've been talking for almost an hour now, and what I see is that you keep using your mind to argue over and over again, and with this, you're just going around in circles.

In our conversation, I find myself repeating, one by one, the advice my therapist Mauricio has been giving me for the past two years. They fit perfectly as responses to Travis's evasive arguments. They seem like a set of instructions tailored to him.

I insist on "the long road," on therapy. He listens to me, and from time to time, when I talk about his wounded child, the beast's bloodshot eyes fill with tears. His inner intelligence accepts what he hears.

Then, he comes back with another "but..." and another one. Until I realize it doesn't make sense to keep refuting his arguments.

I no longer feel like continuing to bear the weight of his low energy. I want to leave. *The only thing I can do at this point* —I tell him—, *is to wish you that tonight, the ayahuasca allows your mind to let go a little more.*

And I end the conversation. I can't, I don't want to convince him. I get up and leave. In a way, I distance myself from my own anger, let it go.

Susan is Susana, really!

I confess that I feel regret for what I am missing out on by not having drunk the glass of San Pedrito.

I know I am missing out on many things: I cannot see, in depth, the magical connection with the souls around me; I have not yet vomited my mother's violent words; I still cannot shed enough tears; last night they barely came out, just as sweat; I am not seeing how far my creativity can go. And this saddens me.

I had and still have the desire to see beyond; to walk perceiving the base of the iceberg; to exchange with these human beings another Family Constellation like the one in the Topanga Canyon ceremony, to write luminous things; I need to continue floating in the Echo of the Universe.

But at the same time, I am proud of myself. I feel more myself than ever. The decision not to drink is today more important to me than the whole universe. This **choosing** is like giving myself my own home; a home where I just want to rest and write; my humble abode.

With the exception of my (somewhat inconsequential?) conversations with the nurse and Travis, what I have done so far was precisely that: rest, and write.

Ahead of me, I see that "Susan", who physically resembles my wife in no way, but who has represented her with such precision. She is a little older than Susana, has Persian features, somewhat dark skin, and a figure matured by the years. Now the possibility of an encounter arises.

The double of Susana heads to a corner of the garden. I stand up and follow her.

Upon approaching her, I ask for permission to speak to her about our "coincidences." Her experience with ayahuasca has been exactly the same as one of my intentions last night: to have a fuller relationship with my wife. The other coincidence was that she was sitting right in front of me.

And excitedly, in English, I add, "My wife even told me that last night, she would be meditating at the same time I was taking ayahuasca, to 'benefit' from my work, since she still doesn't dare to do it. And the funniest thing is that her name is Susana, like you, but with an 'a' at the end."

—Oh, my name is also Susana, with an "a" —she responds in perfect Spanish.

She tells me that she is from Mexico and her husband is from Cuba; that they had divorced some time ago, that they had been separated for seven years, and that a few years ago they got back together and decided never to separate again. This time, although not everything is perfect between them, being together is a true choice.

—And last night I saw both of us together —she continues—, on the couch, entwined in a hug. My husband and I love each other. I work a lot and sometimes he wants us to be closer, since I am very focused on my affairs and do not give him the attention he deserves. From now on, I will try to be more with him, which is what I have chosen.

I say goodbye to Susana, with the strange feeling of having spoken with my wife.

You never finish choosing

I haven't left the house yet. The rest of the weekend, I spent doing what, I reiterate, my Inner Self chose for me in this third experience: resting and writing. That was perhaps the most obvious conclusion of this ceremony.

Also, in these two days, I barely assumed the strength of my adult self who chose not to be swayed by the sexual allure of young Morgan, who sensually wandered around the house threatening to upset my balance. I sought her without seeking her, avoided her unintentionally, in a dance of impossible choreography. Furthermore, the battle between senses and reason resurfaced in each interaction with my companions.

The struggle between desire and choice is recurrent, continuous. I have been so close to betraying all my decisions of this weekend!

Desire returned time and again, with its rapacious flight. And I would argue again: *If I have already chosen not to drink more plants, from my center, now I could, from that same place, "choose" otherwise.*

Having continued taking ayahuasca and San Pedrito would not have been wrong, as I said. There is no right or wrong choice. But precisely, the profound theme of this ceremony was for me the supremacy of choice as such. It substitutes for the very object of choice; precisely because "I am my house."

And when I am, I encounter that Echo of the Universe; that place that appeared before or "between" fears. There, I can, at least for a moment, project happiness until the waters calm, or until I choose when I want to speak to fear. That place where, above all, one can become aware that what we project into the universe is what it returns to us. "Change yourself and the world will change."

It is true that, after the first night of ayahuasca, the following two days were not as revealing and exciting as they would have been under the influence of the sacred cactus. But still, I had deep connections and moments of reflection while talking to others.

I sought to "rest and write." To rest from all the suffering of my childhood traumas, and perhaps from that of my ancestors who sweated for centuries under the injustice of our world. To write with the creativity of my Inner Self, of my Self, of my mind, with my human limitations. It is not necessary to be hyperconnected to the fourth dimension; dozens of Pac-Man pills are not needed to enjoy the game. This is, at least for the moment, what I choose.

Thus, the axis of this whole third experience was, in fact: desire vs. true choice.

At the extreme of desire are the battles we suffer with our addictions; the impulses, the anger, the sadness... But in reality, the path to true choice is a line that has many intermediate points. Only by traversing that line, is one able to choose from our center, from a place aligned and in order.

Once in that place, where no one dwells permanently, one can realize what they truly want; whether this coincides or not with what one desires at a certain moment in life. And thus, act on our choice. From that sacred place where our adult self meets our Inner Wise Self, it will be much easier.

BY WAY OF CONCLUSION
The Result or the Process?

After these three experiences, I noticed that they were distinctly directional. But their apparent disorder later took on, for me, an infinitely ordered sense.

The first one was "vertical, upward," toward that space of Expanded Consciousness from where we all come and to where we all go. Knowing that place not only gave me peace but also the certainty that the sufferings and joys we experience here are nothing more than a game. One that our souls, once, *chose* to play. There I learned that, in the face of fear —which doesn't actually come from outside but from within oneself— there is no need to fight, flee, or resist; it's best to understand, to surrender, let it in.

The second experience was "horizontal," with my peers, with those beings who coincided with me in the ceremony. During its course, the undeniable connections between them and me became apparent. There, the true roots of those bonds that we superficially perceive as "coincidences" in everyday life were revealed to me.

It was an experience that began in Hell itself, but at the same time, it showed me that we are interconnected like stars, with those zodiacal traces that I could clearly glimpse. And in the face of fear, I learned that, if one is willing to surrender, one must pay attention. Because it's not always clear what "surrendering" means in each moment.

This was the only ceremony in which I agreed to take two doses (ayahuasca and San Pedrito); even after having rejected a second day similar to the first. The sacred cactus helped transform that ceremony into a true Family Constellation, in that universe where the traumas of the other participants magically expressed a part of me, as surely as mine expressed parts of them.

The third experience was "inward," into the basement of my subconscious, where all the traumas that condition true choice lie. It was perhaps the most dramatic. That ceremony revealed to me what lies behind the fears caused by family traumas; hidden within them is an energy that wants to break through the barriers of blows, absence, and pain; to break them to emerge like a phoenix. And that underground energy turned out to be, in my case, the feminine side, creativity, which I now use to express myself as a writer.

All three experiences have been revelatory, both of that astral "beyond" from which we will never achieve total knowledge, and of my most personal traumas; and of the happiness and pain of my roots and the human condition. As it became evident, it hasn't been easy to share them.

I've done it for several reasons. One of them, surely, is therapeutic. "Speak your truth, and break," wrote the philosopher Friedrich Nietzsche. The other reason is the hope that my small and partial truths help others look inward, advance in their own paths of self-awareness.

This revelation doesn't necessarily have to come through ayahuasca. There are many ways to access it, alternative paths to travel: from deep meditation or hypnosis to more radical or daring methods, such as those provided by master plants. There is no one that is better or worse than another. And each person internally knows how far they want to go.

To choose our path and our individual measure, we can only listen to our Inner Wise Self. But sometimes we confuse its Voice with that of our mind; we take the critic for a guide. Therefore, in any case, it is essential to always have psychological therapy, whatever it may be, that gives us the tools to remove external influences and discover what we really want. That way, we can decide, in each situation, from our "adult," from our center, and continue advancing on the path of our personal development.

If we choose to try any of these "clues" from the video game, such as ayahuasca, we must consider its distinctive aspect. Unlike other drugs that charge us their price later, it confronts pain head-on. We pay that price in advance, which is an advantage, making it easier and more effective for us to heal and connect.

Still, it sometimes happens that, in the eagerness to reach that place of Expanded Consciousness, or that Echo of the Universe, one wants to continue with one more ceremony. There are people who even seek the pleasure of pain and experience it later as a kind of addiction. It's unlikely to happen, but not impossible.

If, on the other hand, as one would expect, we utilize these substances within a consistent professional framework, the tools provided by therapy will serve as a guide to integrate the teachings of the master plants and interpret the profound understandings they impart to our being.

Ultimately, the most important thing is always to play. The opposite alternative would mean stagnating, regressing, or dying. The goal of life is to advance in the game. And it is up to us to decide if we fulfill it, if we move forward or backward, and at what speed we do it.

The progress is hard and difficult; many times, frustrating. Just when one believes they have overcome something, the next challenge comes (though at another level), and with it, new sufferings. In growth, there is always pain, both our own and others'. As Alfredo, my therapist from adolescence used to say: "When the body grows, the bones hurt; when the mind grows, the soul aches." But, just as it happens at the end of an ayahuasca session, the reward of personal growth, in the medium or long term, is highly beneficial and lasting.

On the other hand, if we decide not to do anything to grow, if we don't acknowledge that we have problems, addictions, etc., if we don't take risks with the aim of changing, if we don't choose the longer path of learning, two things can happen: life's force may enforce change upon us (through illness or unnecessary loss), or the trauma may be passed on to our children and grandchildren, and it will be they who have to endure a pain that doesn't belong to them.

How many of our close relatives are now paying the cost of what our parents or grandparents did and was swept under the rug?

We can also *choose* to do little or "almost nothing." In that case, it's possible that one learns and advances on an almost flat curve for a while. We can choose it, of course. But in that slow progress, it is likely that crises will occur that set us back or even stop us indefinitely. However, if we move forward with self-awareness therapies, the curve will take the desired upward shape, the one we all deserve.

It may happen that with ayahuasca or other "Pac-Man pills" that one may take along the way, we make significant progress in a short period. That's wonderful, but it also carries a risk; that of not fully integrating what has been absorbed.

I have chosen what, for me, is a middle ground: the combination of various dynamics and therapies (psychological, spiritual, meditative), and three doses of ayahuasca. The latter have been (I repeat, for me) like a "doctorate" for all previous therapies; a kind of integration of accumulated learning.

Perhaps I needed a more daring approach. Perhaps I needed to shake off veils too deeply entrenched in my soul and unconscious, due to the resistance –in my case– of reason. Maybe I needed these radical experiences to unleash my creativity and purge deep suffering. And I don't rule out the possibility that I still need more.

But faced with a possible question of whether I would take it again, my answer would be: no. It's not definitive; like nothing in life is. But it's my answer, for now, and that's very important. What funny, isn't it?, to reject ayahuasca after such wonderful experiences.

In the intervals of a year between doses, I have continued working, in my therapy and in my spirit, to apply these teachings in everyday life (something that, I confess, I haven't achieved one hundred percent).

It is quite clear, then, that ayahuasca works at a *psychological* (basement) level. But it also gives us access beyond our subconscious plane. It paves the way for our deep *spiritual* plane; it provides us with direct contact with the Inner Wise Self, who knows everything about us and, in turn, is in contact with everything. (With the player behind the avatar we are?). Also with the Inner Wise One of others, and from there the connections we establish with those around us, those that usually present themselves as "coincidences," lacking an immediate explanation.

Perhaps that spiritual connection that the plant opens for us already has a benefit and healing effect *per se*, even if we don't undergo therapy and don't analyze the reasons and purposes of its revelations. Thus, many people claimed to have cured illnesses, healed relationships, or overcome deep traumas, linked to a spiritual, energetic, or ancestral level.

Regarding the first (subconscious field), I was able to experience that, with the appropriate therapeutic guidance, ingesting ayahuasca has a high benefit for unlocking conflicts and releasing areas entrenched in the past.

And while I cannot testify to the curing of diseases, because that has not been my case, in the spiritual aspect, I witnessed that the "magic" of the master plant provides a certain liberation from weight and pain, including that which we carry for generations. It allows us entry to places like that Zone 2 of Expanded Consciousness, to the Echo of the Universe, or to the space that each one manages to create in their particular experience, among many other manifestations.

Ultimately, ayahuasca, within the framework of my therapeutic process, has been key to advancing on the path of self-awareness and healing. The three experiences were undoubtedly a qualitative leap in my personal growth and development.

And the most wonderful thing about growth curves is that it doesn't matter what level others are at. The only important thing, when a soul chooses to play the game of life, is the purpose of advancing, healing, and smoothing the path for those who come.

If a companion (who in no way competes with you) entered the game at level 8 and exited at level 10, and you entered at level 1 and exited at level 5, your friend advanced two screens, and you, four! That's why, without competition with others, without better or worse, good or bad, what we think or say about others speaks only of ourselves.

Ivan, the shaman who guided me during the second and third ceremonies, said at the end of one of them:

One becomes accustomed to the weight of their backpack, carrying, among other things, multiple stones. They take ayahuasca and leave, knowing they have shed several of them. Initially, they feel lighter —less anxiety, less fear, and so on. Over time, they grow accustomed to the new, albeit lesser, weight of the backpack and may start to believe the work didn't help. Anxiety returns. However, the crucial realization is not to consume more and more ayahuasca but to recognize that it did indeed work; that, in reality, we carry less weight! And that happiness is a state of mind.

The pain never ends. The backpack is never emptied of stones. That's why, and always to each one's measure, we must be clear that the important thing is not the **destination point** (much less the pretense of reaching it). What's important is **the walk.**

A few days ago, I was observing my dogs, Cookie and Brownie, on one of our hikes in the Studio City mountains. In their endless energy, they traverse the path several times, going back and forth, excited by some noise among the plants or some creature they see along the trail. For them, this always represents an opportunity to hunt some small animal. Needless to say, they never catch anything. But the curious thing is that they experience this day in and day out, both in the mountains and at home with the squirrels, and they never get frustrated for not catching any prey. Now I realized the reason is very simple. They don't think about the outcome. They never come back looking bitter (with a dog's face?) saying, "Woof! Darn it! We didn't catch anything." They just enjoy the illusion perhaps, that someday, they will catch something. Or not even that: they just live in the present, the *process* of searching for their prey. And that is enough. They don't even think about the outcome.

The same thing happens when observing any aspect of life. There is no end that justifies the means; because it is **the means** that matter!

When playing a game, the essential thing is not to win or lose (I know, this is a common phrase. But if you think about it), the beauty lies in the **relationship** created between the players.

In any crisis, be it personal, social, or of humanity; in any struggle between two people or groups, the final result doesn't matter. "Your enemy is someone who is sacrificing themselves to show you something you need to learn," I learned from my aunt Ana.

It is precisely for this reason that the destination, the result, or the blessed "end" (which is nothing more than death) don't matter. The key is in the action of **learning**.

It may even be that a player's mission in this game of life is not to reach a certain destination; but I doubt that we don't all have the responsibility to advance. That is, it is possible that a being or soul has decided to incarnate in a person who doesn't want to improve and learn, who shies away from knowing more; that's why free will exists. In fact, this could become inevitable for people who are born with cognitive difficulties, serious or irreversible pathologies, and for someone who is born or falls into a vegetative state. But saving these extreme states, whose levels of consciousness we also don't fully understand, I believe that as long as there is that consciousness, we have **the mission to learn**. Not to reach, win, or achieve a specific end. Only to advance; the more, the better; to be more in touch with our inner wisdom.

In this revealing framework, ayahuasca is a clue on the path of learning. A zoom out to see the game map from above. It's not for everyone, nor is it a foolproof solution. Nor is it even necessary.

Learning is. So that, each time with a little more wisdom, we choose between the forks that the journey presents to us.

And just as you never finish choosing, you never finish feeling some form of pain. You never heal completely. The options are: suffer and repeat, or suffer and learn. There is no other. Well, yes; you can escape by choosing from hundreds of addictions; although it would be almost the same as suffering and repeating.

If we focus on learning, as a natural consequence, we will make better decisions, more in line with our Inner Wise Self, our ethics, our values.

In the simplest of conclusions, it could be said that life is playing, to learn. Everything else is decoration, design.

Perhaps the reader wonders: "So, if you believe you won't take ayahuasca again, and ultimately, these experiences aren't worth as much without the therapeutic framework, do you recommend taking it or not?" Good question. Like a secret code, the answer is hidden in the title of the third experience: "Arriving at the true choice. Desiring and wanting."

Isn't that our true personal challenge?

If you enjoyed this book, found it thought-provoking, or it contributed in any way to your personal growth, I would appreciate it if you could purchase a copy on amazon.com or www.edicionesdeldragon.com and give it to someone you think could benefit from reading it.

You can also send your comments to gp@sucopress.com.

Made in the USA
Las Vegas, NV
04 October 2024

96282385R00134